Alan S. Cole

A descriptive catalogue of a collection of tapestry-woven and embroidered Egyptian textiles

Alan S. Cole

A descriptive catalogue of a collection of tapestry-woven and embroidered Egyptian textiles

ISBN/EAN: 9783741172434

Manufactured in Europe, USA, Canada, Australia, Japa

Cover: Foto ©Thomas Meinert / pixelio.de

Manufactured and distributed by brebook publishing software (www.brebook.com)

Alan S. Cole

A descriptive catalogue of a collection of tapestry-woven and embroidered Egyptian textiles

DEPARTMENT OF SCIENCE AND ART
OF THE COMMITTEE OF COUNCIL ON EDUCATION.

Thomas Wilson,
1218 Connecticut Ave.,
WASHINGTON, D.

A

DESCRIPTIVE CATALOGUE

OF

A COLLECTION OF TAPESTRY-WOVEN AND EMBROIDERED EGYPTIAN TEXTILES

IN THE

SOUTH KENSINGTON MUSEUM.

By ALAN S. COLE.

LONDON:
PRINTED BY EYRE AND SPOTTISWOODE,
PRINTERS TO THE QUEEN'S MOST EXCELLENT MAJESTY,
FOR HER MAJESTY'S STATIONERY OFFICE.
AND SOLD AT THE SOUTH KENSINGTON MUSEUM.

1887.
Price One Shilling.

*** The following will form a section of a Descriptive Catalogue of Tapestries and Embroideries in the South Kensington Museum, now in the press. On account of the interest attaching to the special collection to which it relates, and which has only recently been acquired by the Museum, some copies of this portion are issued beforehand.

South Kensington Museum,
June 1887.

TAPESTRY-WOVEN AND EMBROIDERED EGYPTIAN TEXTILES.

INTRODUCTION.

THE collection of ornamental textiles recently taken rom tombs on the banks of the Nile at Akhmim (Panopolis) 1 Upper Egypt, and purchased for the South Kensington Iuseum, consists of over 300 specimens. Most of them are 1 a state of good preservation in spite of their having lain 1 the tombs or in graves dug in the sand for over thirteen undred years. They offer to both archæologist and antiuarian a wide field for investigation not only in respect of gyptian costume of Roman and Byzantine periods (from st or 2nd century A.D. to 800 A.D.) but also as regards he various influences which gave birth to different styles f ornament. Shedding new light upon a development of ertain artistic textile manufactures and processes, and lustrating survivals and modifications of older ornament, he specimens are of peculiar value in a museum of art anufactures.

A few complete garments have been preserved intact; ut more numerous are the ornamental parts of costumes, f ceremonial cloths, &c. The ornamentations are wrought y means of tapestry weaving and embroidery or needle-ork. Material evidence is thus to hand of the employ-ient of such processes or handicrafts by the Egyptians om the Roman domination down to the conquest of Egypt y the Arabs. Egyptian *polymita* or cloths were, it is said, f the nature of tapestry, while corresponding Babylonian articles were embroidered with the needle.* In the collection we find some specimens of tapestry weaving only, others of tapestry weaving and needlework combined, and others again of needlework alone. Of this last section there are specimens worked with tufts of wool, giving a surface not unlike that of Turkey carpets. The varieties of loom weaving have not been closely examined ; but it may be sufficient here to say that the textiles, apart from their ornamental adjuncts, are of simple weaving with flaxen warp and weft. One class of material is marked by a shaggy or bath towel surface of long loops of flax threads. This possibly is the lighter sort of *gausapum* mentioned by Pliny in his VIII. Book, chapter 73, a quotation from which is given in the Catalogue, p. 4 & 63, with special reference to the specimens there described.

TAPESTRY AND LOOM WEAVING.

As regards the tapestry-weaving process it may be remarked that patterns of many forms, rendered in different coloured threads, are produced with equal skill by artificers in Borneo, in remote Turcoman districts, in China, and in Peru by means of this identical process, facts which possibly point to the conclusion that the comparative simplicity of the process places it in the category of primitive as distinct from more involved arts. It seems therefore to belong more nearly to primitive than to more advanced weaving. The latter shows the influence of mechanical contrivances whereby the weaver may economise his hand labour without diminishing the ornamental effects of his work. Broadly stated, tapestry weaving as a process consists of intertwisting and then pressing down, with a small

---

* *See* Bohn's translation of the Natural History of Pliny (London), 1855. Notes to Book VIII., chap. 74.

comb-like implement or sley, variously coloured threads, which may be silken, woollen, or flaxen, between groups of stretched out warps usually of stouter thread. On the other hand, weaving in a loom with several shuttles, each containing a different coloured set of threads, requires a more elaborate scheme of frame and adjustments than that for tapestry weaving. In the former process shuttles are shot across an entire width of warp threads, although the shuttle threads may have to pass in between a few only of the warps. Rare remnants of Oriental coloured loom weavings, dating probably from the period of the Sassanid dynasty, mechanical arrangements in connexion with looms, imply an use of far more intricate than anything of a similar character in tapestry weaving. The way in which the different shuttles had to be successively thrown between two or more ranks of warp threads points to matured calculation and advanced knowledge in specially employing mechanical contrivances. The same may be said of the system of chanting a hymn or calling out numbers as with Hindus and Japanese, or of pierced cards, as in the Jacquard apparatus, for bringing warp threads of separate ranks into play with the shuttle threads. If a shuttle-woven be compared with a tapestry-woven fabric the difference in the appearance of the textures will be at once seen. A shuttle-woven fabric displays warp and weft threads equally, or nearly so. A tapestry-woven fabric displays close twistings of wefts round warps, which are entirely covered, and not therefore visible in the texture, although they give it a ribbed character. In tapestry weaving one set of warp threads alone is required, and shuttles are not used. Instead of them, several short wooden pegs, each charged with different coloured threads, are employed. The wooden pegs either hang loosely from a beam in front of the worker or are at hand as wanted. He does not depend upon an assistant or special contrivances to regulate the warp, for with his fingers the worker pulls for-

ward the warp threads he requires, between and round
which he twists the coloured threads, and then compacts
his twistings by pressing them down with a small comb-
like instrument. He is indeed under a minimum of
restraint as regards appliances or machinery to regulate his
weaving. Hence the comparative simplicity of the tapestry-
weaving process places its origin at an earlier stage than
that of loom weaving for the production of involved
patterns in many colours. Modern tapestry, that is to say,
tapestry made during the last 500 years, has been worked
in large and small frames standing upon the ground, either
vertically to it (*haute lisse*) or raised horizontally above it
(*basse lisse*). Such frames have always been fitted with
two rollers as wide as the frame,* and one at either end of it.
These rollers between them hold the single rank of warp
threads stretched tightly. The Egyptian tapestry-woven
ornaments, however, are much smaller in size than modern
tapestries, and, as it were, form part of the linens into which
they are woven. The warp threads are those of the linen
itself left, unwoven with weft, in the spaces selected to be
adorned with the tapestry work ; and on the back of most
of the tapestry ornaments in the Egyptian pieces, loose
unwoven weft threads will be seen hanging. Similar spaces
could be obtained by withdrawing the wefts from a fabric
(linen, for instance), and using the warps, which would thus
be left, as the foundation for the subsequent inweaving of
coloured threads. Such a practice indeed seems to be
hinted at in respect of the linen corslet mentioned later on.

---

* In very early weaving, among Hellenic and other races, the strings of the
warp were not kept strained by a lower roller, but each thread of the warp
had a weight attached to it, as is shown in the celebrated Greek vase painting
of Penelope's loom (see woodcut in "A Short History of Tapestry," by
Eugene Muntz, p. 17). Similarly, in Iceland, in 12th century, weights were
used, as in the Fate-web of the Sagas, in which the weights were heroes'
skulls, the shuttle a sword, &c., &c. The many thousands of so-called
spindle-whorls found at Mycenae and Troy, &c. were in many cases weights
for this purpose.—(Note communicated by Professor J. Henry Middleton.)

Withdrawing threads from a fabric is perhaps referred
to in the following quotation from Lucan's Pharsalia,
Book X., ver. 142.* "Her white breasts shine through
" the Sidonian fabric, which, pressed down with the
" comb (or sley) of the Seres, the needle of the Nile work-
" man has separated, and has loosened the warp by stretch-
" ing out (or withdrawing) the weft." At a consider-
ably later date than that of these Egyptian fabrics, and
as a demand arose for larger pieces of tapestry weaving,
the convenience of starting the tapestry making upon
independent ranks of warp threads asserted itself. The
process thereupon became specialised, and large frames
and rollers as previously mentioned came into use ; but, so
far as the peculiar characteristic of twisting coloured threads
upon groups of a single rank of warp threads is concerned,
the method in vogue in Egypt, probably more than two
thousand years ago, is the same as that of the Flemish,
French, English, and other European tapestry making
centres of later and present times ; and it is in such a
connexion as this that the Egyptian tapestries possess
a special interest.

Of the results of twisting coloured threads upon warps,
which are thereby entirely covered with them, something
may be learnt from Herodotus. He writes† of a corslet
sent to Greece by Amasis, the King of the Egyptians, and
describes it as made of linen " with many figures of ani-
" mals inwrought and adorned with gold and cotton wool :
" and on this account each thread of the corslet makes
" it worthy of admiration ; though it is fine it contains
" 360 threads all distinct." Rawlinson's rendering of
this passage is, " The Samians made prize of this corslet

---

* " Candida Sidonio perlucent pectora filo,
  Quod Nilotis acus compressum pectine Serum
  Solvit, et extenso laxavit stamina velo."
† Bohn's Herodotus (London), 1865, and Rawlinson's Herodotus
(London), 1862, vol. 2, Book III., Thalia, chap. 47.

" the year before they took the bowl—it was made of
" linen, and had a vast number of figures of animals in-
" woven into its fabric, and was likewise embroidered with
" gold and tree wool. What is most worthy of admiration
" in it, is, that each of the twists, although of fine texture,
" contains within it 360 threads all of them clearly visible."
It may certainly appear that Herodotus is describing the
appearance of the fine fibres of which a single thread
was composed. But at the present day, and with the
aid of a microscope even, practical experience of the labour
of counting the fibres in a single thread raises a doubt
if either translation gives the meaning Herodotus really
intended to convey. His expression, notwithstanding its
apparent precision, may perhaps have related to the texture
of the corslet rather than to " each thread." The fact that
the corslet was of linen (like many of the Egyptian pieces
now in question) and had animals inwoven into its fabric,
together with the simplicity of the process, favours the sup-
position that it was made in the tapestry-weaving method.
The ribbed appearance of its texture would probably be
such a characteristic as would strike an observer unaccus-
tomed to such things. And he might thereupon proceed
to count the visible ribs, marked by the warp threads, after
he had admired " the figures of animals inwrought and
adorned with gold and cotton wool." A width of 8½ inches
of Egyptian tapestry contains about 180 warp threads.
Hence, if the corslet, which might have been a species of
ephod or breast ornament, had been 17 inches wide, 360
warp threads would have been used in it. In Rawlinson's
Herodotus, Book II., chap. 182, p. 235, an engraving is
given, presumably, of the corslet with figures of animals
which is represented in the tomb of Remeses III. at Thebes.
To some extent a likeness in the heart shapes along the
border and in the animals may be found in some of the
Akhmîm specimens now in the museum. Pliny, nearly
six hundred years after Herodotus, writes of another corslet

or woven breast plate, which was also mentioned by Herodotus in his Book II., chap. 182, and was similar to the one above described. This second corslet had been presented by Amasis to the State of Rhodes, and in Pliny's time was shown in the Temple of Minerva at Lindus as a sacred relic. It had, he says, been almost pulled to pieces by the fingers of numerous visitors who had amused themselves with unravelling the threads to count the 365 threads of which each thread was reported to be made.[*] Whether this is another case of confusion between the fibres of each thread or the threads of the corslet, it is impossible now to say. Specimens with warp threads alone remaining, all the inwoven woollen threads having been eaten away, may be seen in the present collection.

The earliest date proposed for a few of the Egyptian textiles now before us, is about the first or 2nd century A.D. It is therefore within the range of probabilities that they are merely survivals of similar works made 500 years earlier. Another circumstance which perhaps may help to fix the age of these Egyptian examples is found in the use of wools and flax to the exclusion of silk, and this, notwithstanding that the elaborate ornamentation bespeaks the production of these articles for persons of consideration and wealth.

THE USE OF SILK.

Records concerning the introduction into the Roman market of limited supplies of silk stuffs for the use of the most wealthy classes, occur in the writings of poets in the Augustan age. Sumptuary edicts and early Christian austerity in simplicity of costume, however, operated to restrict the employment of silk during the few subsequent centuries, and apparently it is not until the reign of

---

[*] Pliny, Book XIX., chap. 2.

Justinian (A.D. 530), that a more extended use of silk arose, and has since then flourished in Europe. Had silks, which are seen in rare fragments of woven and embroidered materials dating from Byzantine periods, been generally available, it is perhaps fair to surmise that they would have been readily used by the skilful Copts of Egypt, to whose hands we trace the works under discussion.

PATTERNS.

Suggestions are occasionally given in the Catalogue of the possible sources from which the patterns for these specimens may have been derived. Scarcely any possess the purity of treatment which is characteristic of the Periclean period in Greece. Nevertheless there are specimens showing a direct relationship to the matured ornament of such an epoch. Many of the designs are obviously due to Roman influences, and seem to belong more closely to a date after the better works of art had ceased to be produced for the Romans, and when a school of poor imitators was springing into existence, such as that either of Roman Christians or painstaking Byzantines. In squares of ornaments occur patterns based upon a geometric arrangement of curved and interlacing stems which serve as a framework or setting to figures, of crouching men bearing shields, of centaurs, of mounted hunters, baskets of fruit, floral devices and other details. In treatment these are almost identical with patterns of Roman mosaic pavements from and after the 1st century. Besides these, and of a type like that of panelled figures in Pompeian mural decoration, there are squares containing most delicately worked, though poorly drawn half length representations of Hermes and Apollo, the titles being in Greek letters of a late character, perhaps 3rd or 4th century. Then, there are other specimens in which the treatment of animals, running one behind the other with expressive action, affords evidence of a percolation into Egypt of long lived and early Assyrian and Phœnician styles of design. The forms which later modifications of such designs assumed, may be seen in the carved ivory horns or oliphants ascribed to Byzantine sources of the 9th and 11th centuries. Indian metal workers at the present day use similar ornaments for the inlay of blades. Another distinctive class of pattern is that of intertwining stems or bands arranged into rectangular and polygonal shapes, elaborate star forms, &c. These should be compared with Saracenic ornament, composed of somewhat similar devices. The guilloche border, the key or fret pattern used as a surface or diapering ornament, the Greek wave ornament and waved stems with ivy leaves, and with vine leaves, recur again and again in the Egyptian textiles. A totally distinct class of designs consists of groupings of ill-proportioned human beings, mostly wearing aureoles or *nimbi*. These illustrate scriptural events in a primitive style like that of certain of the coloured scratched slabs from the catacombs in the Lateran Museum at Rome. Amongst them sainted personages, such as St. George, St. Mark, St. Demetrius, and others, held in reverence by the Christian Copts, are to be traced in some of the broader bands of bright coloured tapestry weavings.* But it is only by studying the specimens themselves that one can form an adequate idea of the different classes of pattern.

COSTUME.

The complete robes, with sleeves and skirts, belong to the tunic class, and are not unlike dalmatics, and even heralds' tabards of mediæval times. Some were possibly used for ecclesiastical purposes, others are merely decorated secular costumes.

---

* Kermes, red dye, is frequently used in these (see Bands, No. 734-1886, p. 14, 732-1886, p. 15, 863-1886, p. 16; Cuff, 723-1886, p. 32; Panel, 722-1886, p. 38, &c.). This splendid colour was got from the little beetle that feeds on the ilex-oaks of Greece and Asia Minor, and was also much used in fine Persian carpets.

The tunic of the Greeks and Romans was an under-dress, over which a cloak (or himation or toga) was worn. With the Egyptians of the Roman and perhaps earlier periods, it would appear that the tunic, of the cut displayed in the Museum specimens, was a robe or dress, loose and easily opened, as was suitable for use in the warm climates of Middle and Upper Egypt, and worn alone without any additional outer garment. The towel-faced material when used for costume was, according to Dr. Karabacek, worn in the winter. In the height of summer, when steeped in fresh water, the peasants would use it to wrap round the wine amphoræ to cool their contents. This rough material, although one specimen at least shows us that it was made for wealthy wearers, seems to have later on been adopted by peasants and field labourers. To return therefore to the more costly tunics, the bands or *clavi* (wide and narrow), crossing each shoulder, and running vertically down the front and back of the robe, are analogous in shape to, though more ornate than, those usually seen in Roman costumes of the third and fourth centuries, and later. Amongst the bands are a few, the ends of which are round, each finishing with a little pendent panel. The position in which the bands were worn suggests a possible relationship to the deacons' "orarion," as distinguished from the "epitrachelion" (*see* Butler, *Ancient Coptic Churches*, Vol. II., for information as to vestments).

Square panels (*adjunctae tabulae*) are sometimes placed one on each arm just beyond the *clavi*, as well as upon the back and front of the skirt. Medallions (*orbiculi*) are similarly used, but in conjunction with *clavi* or bands rounded at the ends, and terminating in small oval panels. This last named class of ornaments thus seem to be later variants of the squares and square-ended bands; and it may be a matter worth investigation whether the tunic with square-ended bands and often with a sort of breast and

back panel or ephod, close up to the neck, is not a survival of Egyptian costume in Ptolemaic and earlier times;
and whether this fashion in ornamenting robes was not
rather transplanted to Rome than, as has been suggested,
that the Copts obtained their ideas from Roman and
Byzantine fashions.

CONTEMPORARY PAPYRI.

Some light may perhaps be thrown upon the ethnical
character of the Egyptian tapestry weavings and embroideries, from the papyri discovered at El-Fayûm,
which are now preserved at Vienna, and are known
as the Theodore Graf find. Dr. Karabacek published
a lecture upon them delivered in 1883. He stated
that the oldest of the papyri is dated 487 A.D., whilst
the latest is dated 909 A.D. Between these dates is
an array of writings in six languages, namely, Greek,
Coptic, Hebrew, Arabic, Sassanid-Persian (Pehlevi), and
Syriac. This variety of languages points to the politi-
cal changes in the national life of Egypt during the 400
years referred to; or, as Dr. Karabacek says, "to put
" it differently, so far as the ethnographical relations of
" Egypt are concerned, there arises as from a panorama
" and out of the motley turmoil of civil commotion, the
" Greek state hastening to its complete decline, as it
" engages in conflict with the newly budding culture of the
" Arabs."

But still more valuable, in the present case, are Dr.
Karabacek's remarks upon the textiles which also are part
of the Theodore Graf find. Judging from the descriptive
catalogue, and in the absence of a comparison of specimens
in the Graf, with those in the South Kensington Collections,
it seems that the latter includes a greater number of textile
ornaments, of earlier date, such as I have ventured to call
Egypto-Roman, than the former.

TAPESTRY WEAVING BY COPTS.

The information as to the actual locality whence the Graf specimens were taken is at present meagre. But it is well established that they were exhumed from burial places either in the neighbourhood of El-Fayûm in Middle Egypt, or that of Akhmîm (Chemmis or Panopolis) in Upper Egypt. Those in the South Kensington collection came from Akhmîm. Precisely similar tapestry weavings and embroideries in the British Museum also come from Akhmîm, as well as from the Arab village of Sakkarah, near Memphis. Hence there is conclusive proof that the same character of textile workmanship and styles of pattern or design existed at places remote from one another along the Nile. This pervading similarity in character receives corroboration and explanation from the fact that the area occupied by the Copts was in the valley and delta of the Nile, from Assouan to the Mediterranean. The Copts may be regarded as the inheritors and perpetuators of ancient Egyptian talent in all classes of handiwork. They were, and to a large extent are, the skilled workmen of many Egyptian towns. Weaving and cognate processes were amongst the other handicrafts practised by them. Of notable Coptic towns Akhmîm (Chemmis or Panopolis) may be cited, though of course there were many others, such as Coptos, and again farther north along the banks of the Nile. Of Panopolis, which in Ptolemaic times was distinguished for the productions of its weavers, Herodotus wrote that its inhabitants were the "only Egyptians" not remarkable for their abhorrence of Greek customs. In thus speaking of these Egyptians he was, of course, referring to the same people as those which later we call Copts. Whilst the Coptic temperament seems to have favoured a conservative tendency in preserving the traditions of various branches of handicraft or manufacture, it was nevertheless peculiarly sensitive to new influences; a trait which is brought out by the eagerness with which the Christian religion was adopted by the Copts. In the same way would the Copts be susceptible to the influences of new shapes, and patterns, which commerce or foreign domination brought before them.

FOREIGN INFLUENCES ACTING UPON COPTS.

Akhmim, which is at present the most southerly of the districts or towns from which textiles and embroideries of the peculiar class now being discussed have been obtained, is on the east bank of the Nile, half way between Thebes, on the south, and Assiout, on the north. Coptos, about thirty miles north of Thebes, and more than twice that distance south of Akhmim (Panopolis), was, in Ptolemaic and early Roman times, an important town on the route of the Arabian, Persian, and Indian commerce with Alexandria. Grecian and Roman merchandise arriving at Coptos was taken by Arab carriers across the desert to the coast of the Red Sea, and so transhipped at Berenice, not far from Suakin, for conveyance to the east. Influences from such commerce would naturally be felt at a place of the importance of Akhmîm (Panopolis), as well as elsewhere along the Nile route. When Panopolis was notable for its Coptic weavers, Greeks, and after them Romans, were to be found in many of the southern towns of the Thebaid. Strabo accompanied the Roman prefect Aelius Gallus on a tour up the Nile as far as Syene (Assouan) the border town of Egypt and Ethiopia. In many of the towns between Syene and Alexandria were Roman garrisons and Greek and Roman inhabitants. Two hundred years later, however, the limits of Roman domination in this district began to shrink, and rebellions against it on the part of Copts and Arabs occurred. Coptos was besieged and destroyed by Diocletian, with little purpose as a check to the gradual pushing out of the Romans by Copts, Nubians, and Arabs. Roman domination in Egypt which had succeeded that of the Greeks, in some 600 years dwindled away under a short period of Sassanid-Persian power during the reign of King Chosroes II., and a longer and more persistent supremacy of Arab Mohammedanism.

These very brief notes may perhaps serve the present purpose of indicating how it was that the Coptic tapestry makers and embroiderers should have produced patterns of Greek and Roman character. The survival of such patterns, intermixed later on with Christian Coptic emblems and figures, the cross, the fish, saints, and so forth, finds something of a parallel in what took place in Rome in the early days of Christianity, when symbols and rites of the Mithraic religion were frequently used by Christians; symbols and rites remaining almost unchanged externally, though conveying to the Christian adapters a new meaning, different from that of their Pagan originators.

Many of the specimens bear traces of what may be termed Persian or Oriental influences in design and pattern, which seem to show themselves in the satisfactory and well balanced distribution of forms and details, closely fitted into a given space. A group of birds or animals facing one another, with a tree or emblem between each pair, although of frequent occurrence in classes of Persian and Saracenic patterns, is a distinctive Assyrian design. Its survival and widespread introduction into Europe are no doubt very much due to Persian works of art. Some examples of it will be seen in the Egyptian textiles, and these possibly are to be connected with the short period when Sassanid-Persian rule was in the ascendant; though commerce with Persia and Oriental countries, during a much longer space of time, had probably done a great deal more not only towards diffusing such influences in Egypt, but in carrying them to Byzantium.

CLASSIFICATION OF SPECIMENS.

The classification of specimens into Egypto-Roman, Christian-Coptic, and Egypto-Byzantine, as well as the ascription of periods when the articles were made, may no doubt wear a look of empiricism. The attempt has been made with a sense of incomplete information too hastily gathered under pressure of time. It is, however, hoped that it may instigate the production of more definite knowledge in this direction.

In conclusion, I should say that whilst cataloguing the specimens now exhibited in the South Kensington Museum, I have had the advantage of most valuable suggestions from Mr. William Morris, Professor Middleton (Slade Professor at Cambridge), Mr. A. J. Butler (author of Ancient Coptic Churches), Mr. A. Higgins and others. Some samples of the material have been chemically tested by Professor Japp, F.R.S., and botanically investigated by Dr. Scott, of the Normal School of Science, who have found that the woven threads with which the robes and cloths are made are of various qualities of flax.

May 1887.   ALAN S. COLE.

CATALOGUE.

(a.) TUNICS and ROBES with bands (clavi), and square
and circular panels (adjunctæ tabulæ).

TUNIC of linen, with bands across the shoulders, ornaments
on breast and back, and squares on front skirt of
woven tapestry, brown and red wools, and yellow flax.
From ancient tombs at Akhmîm (Panopolis), Upper
Egypt. ? Egypto-Roman. ? 3rd to 6th centy. L. about
3 ft. 6 in., W. about 4 ft. 3 in. Bought (631 to 922, 300l.).
633.–1886.

The pattern on the bands over the shoulders consists of linked
roundels formed by intertwining small leaf stems. In the roundels
are geometric ornaments alternated with different animals. Similar
bands of ornament cross the breast and the back ; along their lower
edge are dentated shapes, from which depend pointed panels and small
figures. These panels, back and front, are filled in with grotesque, cross
legged naked figures with uplifted hands, some in red, some in black
wool. The lower parts of the shoulder bands are of triple bands, the
outer ones of waved stem with vine leaves and bunches, the centre ones
of guilloche ornament; each of these terminate in pendent vases or vine
leaves. The vases are of bulkier shape than those which, in other specimens, seem to bear a mark more distinctive of earlier Roman origin. The
pattern on the squares on shoulders consist of a St. George's and St. Andrew's cross combined and repeated in four octagons, which are inclosed
by a bordering of leaf medallions, within which are degraded renderings
of animals and birds. The squares on the skirt have one cross in an
octagon, set in a similar bordering as described for other squares. The
back and sleeves of this robe are much eaten away.

TUNIC of linen, with ornaments of woven tapestry, brown
wool, and yellow flax, consisting of bands across shoulders
and down whole length of skirt, back and front. The pattern consists of a series of lions, dogs, ibexes or goats
Between these bands and about the neck, on chest and
back are oblong panels, filled in with four naked male
figures (? Ethiopians) in various positions, two carrying
offerings in their uplifted right hands, one carrying a
leaf stem, another with a staff, and all bearing shields
on their left arms, with upturned faces. The double

bands on each cuff are smaller versions of the bands along
the length of the robe. From ancient tombs at Akhmîm
(Panopolis), Upper Egypt. ? Egypto-Roman. ? 3rd to
6th centy. L. about 3 ft. 4 in., W. about 4 ft. 5 in.
Bought (631 to 922, 300l.). 631.–1886.

The absence of ornamental compartments in which the figures and
animals might have been placed, as in other specimens, together with
the absence of square panels on shoulders or on skirts as well as the
shape of the tunic, although undoubtedly like the dalmatic robe not
generally adopted in Rome until after the reign of Commodus, might
point to an earlier origin even than one between 1st to 6th centuries,
which is the date assigned to band 786.–1886. In band No. 660 somewhat similar animals are set in roundels. On the shoulder at centre of
the bands is a roundel containing a cross.

TUNIC of linen, with ornaments of woven tapestry, red wool,
and yellow flax, consisting of a narrow band across the
shoulders, back and front, with a serpent (?) and small
rosettes, and terminating in a small trefoil. On the
shoulders and lower portions of skirts are small red
squares with a large yellow rosette in centre, and small
ones at the corners. The bands on sleeves are similar
to those on body of robe. From ancient tombs at
Akhmîm (Panopolis), Upper Egypt. ? Egypto Byzantine.
? 3rd to 9th centy. L. about 4 ft., W. about 3 ft. Bought
(631 to 922, 300l.). 632.–1886.

The simplicity of the ornamentation on this robe possibly indicates
that it was made for a person less wealthy or of less consideration than
those who used much more elaborately patterned robes. Following a
suggestion given by the learned Dr. Karabacek in his catalogue of the
Th. Graf discoveries in Egypt, a comparison may be made between
the small squares containing rosettes, above mentioned, and similar
ornament upon the robe of an Apollo or David figured in a Greek MS.
Psalter of the 10th century engraved in Bordier's Manuscrits Grecs de
la Bibliotheque Nationale de Paris. 1883.

TUNIC (short, without sleeves) of linen, decorated with two
bands, back and front, across the shoulders (of repeated
formal stem and leaf devices, set between scallop edges)
of woven tapestry, brown wool, and yellow flax. The
lower borders are fringed. From ancient tombs at
Akhmîm (Panopolis), Upper Egypt. ? Egypto-Byzantine.
? 3rd to 9th centy. L. about 3 ft. 4 in., W. about 1 ft.
9 in. Bought (631 to 922, 300l.). 636.–1886.

This is a short robe, without sleeves, and open at the sides.

TUNIC of linen (very decayed condition), with round ended
bands over shoulders; oblong panels, back and front,

about neck between them ; on shoulders and cuffs, square
panels ; along the edge of the skirt, and at the ends of it,
bands similar to those over shoulders; upon the skirt
square panels. All these ornaments of woven tapestry,
dark blue wool, and yellow flax. The pattern consists
chiefly of ornamental roundels, in which are debased
figures of animals and human beings. *Egypto-Byzantine.*
? 3rd to 9th centy. Bought, 3*l.* 270.–1886.

The rude and debased character of the ornaments may be noted if
specimens such as No. 631, 632, and 633 be compared with this.

TUNIC of linen (very decayed condition), with round ended
bands and pendants over shoulders, and circular panels on
shoulders and skirt, of woven tapestry, coloured wools
and flax, worked separately and applied to the tunic.
The ornament consists of groups of human beings—some
with nimbi—animals and ornaments of floral forms.
? Christian Coptic ? 6th to 9th centy. Bought, 3*l.*
271.–1886.

The woven tapestry ornaments do not form part of the texture of
this robe, as is the case with No. 631 and 633. The warp threads are
small, hence the texture of the weaving is of comparatively fine quality.
The character of this kind of ornamentation and work may be seen in
the better specimens, such as No. 734.–1886; and circular panel 743.–
1886.

TUNIC of linen (very decayed condition), with bands and
other fragments of woven tapestry in coloured wools and
flax, worked separately and applied to the tunic. The
ornament consists of human figures, animals, and orna
mented borders. *? Christian Coptic.* ? 6th to 9th centy.
Bought, 3*l.* 272.–1886.

The pattern on the bands is like that in No. 848. See somewhat
similar treatment in 741 and 866. Portions of the bands in this robe
are well preserved; but they and all the woven tapestry ornament
belonged formerly to some other robe, and do not form part of the
texture of the robe, as is the case with Nos. 631 and 633.

TUNIC of linen (very decayed and fragmentary condition),
with round ended bands and circular panels of woven
tapestry, coloured wools and flax, worked separately and
applied to the tunic. The ornament is of very debased
forms. *? Christian Coptic.* ? 6th to 9th centy. Bought,
2*l.* 273.–1886.

See similar and better preserved circular panels No. 855 and 855A.

Tunic of linen (? for a woman), with ornament, on sleeves and across shoulders, back and front, down the whole length of the robe, of finely woven tapestry in coloured wools ; consisting of double rows of flower buds,* between which are detached rosettes of yellow blossom on black roundel. From ancient tombs at Akhmîm (Panopolis), Upper Egypt. ? 6th to 9th centy. L. about 3 ft., W. about 4 ft. 4 in. Bought (631 to 922, 300*l*.),

634.-1886.

* See similar buds in the robe of St. Agnese's figure in mosaic in the church of St. Agnes beyond the walls, at Rome ; see also 739.—1886.

Sleeve, shoulder, and part of the breast of a linen robe, of rough towel material faced with flax loops, with bands (two intact, one with wool eaten away) and a circular panel, of woven tapestry, brown wool, and yellow flax. The pattern in the circle consists of a dancing figure, with hat and stick, (? Mercury) apparently grasping the head of a seated woman, and surrounded by a radiating leaf or cone border of a type similar to that seen in Assyrian sculpture; the ornament in the bands is a waved stem and long oval leaves and a fish. From ancient tombs at Akhmîm (Panopolis), Upper Egypt. ? 1st to 6th centy. About 2 ft. 2 in. by 2 in. Bought (631 to 922, 300*l*.). 760.-1886.

The simplicity of style of this ornament in this specimen seems to give it an earlier date than that of other specimens. Pliny writes, "The " gausapa has been brought into use in my father's memory, and I " myself recollect the amphi malla" (probably with a shaggy nap on both sides) "and the long shaggy apron being introduced; but at the " present day the laticlave tunic is beginning to be manufactured in " imitation of the gausapa." The ornament in the band can be best seen with light behind it.

(*b*.) BANDS [wide and narrow (*Latus clavus, Angustus clavus*)] for robes, chiefly tunics of the dalmatic class.

Bands (fragments of) and Breast Panel (of woven tapes-try, coloured wools, and yellow flax, for a linen robe. The ornament of the bands consists of buds and blossoms and small roundels placed between two narrow bands of waved stem and leaf ornament. Between the pendants marking the divisions of the breast ornament are figures with shields and two sets of three formal hanging lotus

5

flowers. From ancient tombs at Akhmîm (Panopolis),
Upper Egypt. ? 1st centʸ. About 14¼ in. by 11 in.
Bought (631 to 922, 300*l.*). 769.-1886.

These lotus flowers furnish the only instance amongst these specimens
from Akhmîm of influence of early Egyptian ornament. Their appearance
in conjunction with the human figures is interesting, since similar human
figures appear in specimens where ornament apparently of other origin and
periods is used.

BAND (portion of) for a linen robe, of woven tapestry, blue-
black wool and yellow flax with (?) a Gorgon head at
centre of band, delicately wrought in coloured wools.
The pattern, divided at centre by the head, placed in a
roundel, consists of a series of circular and oblong panels,
of which latter there are one each side of the Gorgon
head. In the one is a rudely drawn naked male figure
playing on a pipe with formal tree ornament on each side
of line; in the other (?) a flying figure of Victory with
wreath in her hand (bracelets and bangles at wrists
and ankles). Beyond both these oblong panels are three
linked roundels containing animals (lion, bear, ibex, and
dogs). Similar roundels terminate the band at both
ends; and between the sets of roundels are oblong panels
containing grotesque naked men, one (with bracelets and
bangles at wrists and ankles) bearing a red staff (? a
sceptre), the other a spear. From ancient tombs at
Akhmîm (Panopolis), Upper Egypt. *Egypto-Roman.*
? 1st to 6th centʸ. About 3 ft. 9 in. by 5 in. Bought
(631 to 922, 300*l.*). 786.-1886.

The Gorgon head, for quality of weaving, drawing, and colouring, is
superior to other parts of this band; see similar weaving in Nos. 651, 652,
and 653, in respect of material, treatment, and colour. It marks the place
where the band was to be hung on the shoulder. It suggests a Roman
influence in treatment. The figure of Victory, taken in conjunction with
that of the man bearing a staff or sceptre, may suggest that the band was
made for some Roman chief. The plan of linking the panels and
roundels together is similar to that of many Roman patterns (for pavements, &c.) of the best and later periods. The date assignable to this
piece is possibly as early as the 1st centʸ.

BAND AND MEDALLION (fragments) for a linen robe, of
woven tapestry and needlework, brown wool and yellow
flax. The ornament on the band consists of a vertical
series of human beings and animals. Amongst the former
are a man with a circular shield on his left arm, and a
dancing woman (?) with drapery thrown across her right
shoulder and girdled about her waist, and a similarly
male draped figure leaning on a staff. The medallion
contains a group: two figures, a female with her arm

round the neck of (?) a king, in a chariot drawn by two centaurs, one playing a pipe or trumpet, the other bearing a bowl, while above, right and left, a figure holding a goblet and one playing (?) a drum: in between the figures is a delicate stem and leaf ornament. From ancient tombs at Akhmim (Panopolis), Upper Egypt. *Egypto-Roman.* ? 1st to 5th cent^y. About 2 ft. 3 in. by 8¾ in. Bought (631 to 922, 300*l.*). 784.–1886.

For variety of figures, and pourtrayal of action and gesture, especially in respect of the figures on the band, which seem to be versions of classic sculpture, this specimen is remarkable. It compares with No. 786.–1886, in which the Roman origin seems to assert itself.

BAND AND SQUARE (portion of) for a child's linen robe, of woven tapestry, brown wool, yellow flax; the pattern of the band consists of a formal series of ivy leaves and other waved stem ornament. The square contains a figure kneeling on left knee, and floating drapery at back; on his right leg he rests (?) a bird; this group in brown upon a circular space of yellow is set within a border of ivy leaves. From ancient tombs at Akhmim (Panopolis), Upper Egypt. *Egypto-Roman.* ? 1st and 5th cent^y. About 18½ in. by 6 in. Bought (631 to 922, 300*l.*). 706.–1886.

BAND (narrow) AND MEDALLION for a child's linen robe, of woven tapestry, brown wool and yellow flax. The part of the band to lay on the shoulder is a strip of plain brown, with three circles outlined upon it. The ends of the band consist of a vertical series of two-handled amphora-shaped vases, each surmounted with a vine leaf. The medallion (which also rested on the shoulder) encloses a double-handled amphora-shaped vase, with vine stem and leaves springing from each side of its mouth and encircling it. The detail on vases and the fibres in leaves are of needlework. From ancient tombs at Akhmim (Panopolis), Upper Egypt. ? 1st to 5th cent^y. About 2 ft. 3 in. by 4½ in. Bought (631 to 922, 300*l.*). 650.–1886.

Such circular panels, used to decorate various parts, the shoulders, fronts, and skirts of robes, are to be seen in late Roman or early Byzantine costumes. An analogous fashion prevails with the Chinese in the decoration of robes. The present specimen is remarkable for the minuteness and carefulness of its design and its completeness.

BAND (narrow) AND SQUARE for a child's linen robe, of woven tapestry, brown and yellow wools. The band consists of thick twisted stem ornament, with leaves

occasionally introduced. The square has a scalloped
ornamental edging which frames a circular yellow space
upon which is a figure representing (?) a peacock in
brown. From ancient tombs at Akhmîm (Panopolis),
Upper Egypt. *Egypto-Roman.* ? 1st to 5th cent^y.
About 2 ft. 4 in. by 1 in. Bought (631 to 922, 300*l.*).

680.–1866.

The peacock's crest is indicated, but his tail consists of one large peacock's feather.

BAND (end of) for a linen robe, of woven tapestry, dark blue
wool and yellow flax. The pattern consists of a vertical
series of two scroll-handled amphora-shaped vases with
formal leafed sprigs, blue on yellow. From ancient
tombs at Akhmîm (Panopolis), Upper Egypt. ? *Egypto-
Roman.* ? 1st to 5th cent^y. About 21½ in. by 3 in.
Bought (631 to 922, 300*l.*). 913.–1886.

The shape of these vases suggests a Roman origin for the pattern.

BAND (fragment of, from a linen robe) of woven tapestry,
dark blue wool, and yellow flax, the edges are indented
with semi-circular forms and spots; down the centre are
rows of double-handled amphora-shaped vases with trefoil
or fleurs-de-lys sprays. From ancient tombs at Akhmîm
(Panopolis), Upper Egypt. ? *Egypto-Roman.* ? 1st to
5th cent^y. About 8¼ in. by 3½ in. Bought (631 to 922,
300*l.*). 914.–1886.

BAND (portion of) for a linen robe, of woven tapestry, brown
wools and yellow flax. The pattern consists of a vertical
series of two-handled amphora-shaped vases, with two
ivy leaves in each: brown on yellow. From ancient
tombs at Akhmîm (Panopolis), Upper Egypt. *Egypto-
Roman.* ? 1st to 5th cent^y. About 2 ft. 1½ in. by 2¼ in.
Bought (631 to 922, 300*l.*). 649.–1886.

These are more rudely drawn than the vases in 913.–1886. Towards
one end of the band is a diamond shape marking the spot which was
placed on the shoulder, with the ornament hanging vertically on both
sides of it.

BAND (portion of) for a linen robe, of woven tapestry, black
wool and yellow flax. The pattern consists of a vertical
series of two scroll-handled amphora-shaped vases, with
formal leaf sprigs, black on yellow. At one end is a
Maltese cross within a circle.† From ancient tombs at
Akhmîm (Panopolis), Upper Egypt. ? *Egypto-Roman.*
? 1st to 6th cent^y. About 2 ft. 6¼ in. by 1½ in. Bought
(631 to 922, 300*l.*). 834.–1886.

† This marks the half of the orignal band, and was the spot where the
band was placed on the shoulder. See also 913, 1886.

8

BAND (portion of) for linen robe, of woven tapestry, brown
and yellow wools and flax. The pattern consists of two
intertwisting stems forming a series of oval panels, in
which, on yellow ground, are ornamental tree devices
alternated with every two panels, each of which latter has
either a lion and a hare or a lion and an ibex figured
on it. From ancient tombs at Akhmîm (Panopolis), Upper
Egypt. *Egypto-Byzantine.* ? 5th to 9th centy. About
21 in. by 4 in. Bought (631 to 922, 300*l*.). 660.-1886.

The treatment of the animals is suggestive of that to be met with in
carved ivory horns or oliphants of the 9th and 11th centuries, such as
the Byzantine horn, No. 7953.-1862, in the collection of ivories. But
similar animals in sequence are to be frequently seen figured upon
Assyrian sculptures of the 8th century, B.C.

BAND (portion of) for linen robe, of woven tapestry, blue
wools and yellow flax. The pattern consists of repeated
circles containing representations of animals (lion,
(?) long-eared Abyssinian dog, and ibex) worked in blue
on yellow ground, with red tongues. From ancient tombs
at Akhmîm (Panopolis), Upper Egypt. ? 3rd to 9th centy.
About 13 in. by 4 in. Bought (631 to 922, 300*l*.).
661.-1886.

BAND (portion of) for linen robe, of woven tapestry, brown
wool and yellow flax. The pattern consists of a vertical
series of nude human figures* (? Ethiopian) in different
postures. One holding a shield, another a staff at the back
of his neck, with a mantle falling over both shoulders,
another with uplifted left hand, his right resting upon a
club (this figure is almost entirely eaten away); alternating
with the figures are long-horned and long-eared animals
and grotesque animal forms. The edges of the band are
of small scalloped pattern. From ancient tombs at
Akhmîm (Panopolis), Upper Egypt. *? Egypto-Roman.*
? 1st to 5th centy. About 3 ft. 10¼ in. by 4 in. Bought
(631 to 922, 300*l*.). 788.-1886.

* The treatment of the figures seems to display a Greco-Roman influence,
whilst the curly hair of the figures seems to suggest that they are Ethiopians.
See somewhat similar figures in Robe 631.-1886.

BAND (portion of) for linen robe, of woven tapestry, brown
wool and yellow flax. The pattern consists of a series
of rectangular panels, edged on outer sides with a small
trefoil ornament. In the panels are, alternately, mer-
maids or syrens playing (?) a sort of Pan's pipe, and
nude male figures in different postures; the uppermost
one playing a flute—the next a Pandean pipe—the

next is almost untraceable—the next with a pendent ornament from his neck and belt round his waist, dancing—the next a repetition of the first, and the last dancing, with both hands uplifted and a scarf hanging beneath them. From ancient tombs at Akhmîm (Pano- polis), Upper Egypt. *? Egypto-Roman.* ? 1st to 5th centy. About 2 ft. 6 in. by 4 in. Bought (631 to 922, 300*l.*). 790.–1886.

. See also 788.–1886 and 633.–1885. The type of face and hair suggests the Ethiopian.

BANDS (two, part of), of woven tapestry, brown and red wools, and yellow flax, for a linen robe. The bands are edged with small trefoil ornament, between which are a series of roundels. In these, alternately, are tree and leaf devices well distributed within the roundel—and naked male figures in different postures: one holding a crook in his right hand and an ivy spray in his left; another carrying off a long basket of fruit (red); another with a crook over his left shoulder and carrying (?) a pail in his right; another carrying a duck in both hands; another bearing a musical instrument or Pan's pipes.† From ancient tombs at Akhmîm (Panopolis), Upper Egypt. *? Egypto-Roman.* ? 1st to 5th centy. About 2 ft. 8 in. by 18 in. Bought (631 to 922, 300*l.*). 656.–1886.

See also †790.–1886, where syrens are playing on similar instruments.

BAND (portion of) for a linen robe, of woven tapestry, dark blue and yellow wools. The pattern consists of linked roundels, alternately filled with a naked figure holding a crook in his left and a branch in his right hand, a scarf falling from his right shoulder; and a formal spreading tree ornament. From ancient tombs at Akhmîm (Panopolis), Upper Egypt. *Egypto-Roman.* ? 1st to 5th centy. About 13¼ in. by 3¾ in. Bought (631 to 922, 300*l.*). 656*a.*–1886.

See also 656.–1866.

BAND (part of) of a robe of rough towel-faced material, of woven tapestry, brown, red, and blue wools, and yellow flax, with naked female figures in different actions, one holding two pairs of (?) ring rattles; another with (?) two scarfs*; alternated with a lion and ibex. From ancient tombs at Akhmîm (Panopolis), Upper Egypt. ? 3rd to 9th centy. About 18 in. by 8 in. Bought (631 to 922, 300*l.*). 783.–1886.

* See similar form in 656 and 656A.–1886.

BAND (portion of) for a linen robe, of woven tapestry, purple and white wools. The pattern consists of linked roundels, in which are alternately naked human figures, in different postures, and animals. The links between the roundels are filled in with ducks. A formal tree ornament, similar to that in (786.–1886), occurs in all the roundels, beyond and between which is a vase with branching floral ornament. From ancient tombs at Akhmîm (Panopolis), Upper Egypt. ? 1st to 6th cent^y. About 3 ft. 10½ in. by 5½ in. Bought (631 to 922, 300*l*.).
789.–1886.

BANDS (pair of, with round ends and pendants,) for a linen robe, of woven tapestry, formerly filled in with ground of red wool, the ornament in yellow flax still remaining. The pattern in centre of each band consists of a long panel, above and below which is a series of three circular panels, each containing a bird or animal. In each of the long panels is a grotesque man or figure with two limbs (? legs) outstretched on one side, and an arm and hand holding a bird on the other. The edges to each band are of repeated vertical floral devices and circular forms with a straight stem running through them. From ancient tombs in Akhmîm (Panopolis), Upper Egypt. *Christian Coptic.* ? 6th to 9th cent^y. About 2 ft. 1 in. by 9½ in. Bought (631 to 922, 300*l*.). 721.–1886.

See similar coloured tapestry in Nos. 826.–896 and 888.–1886.

BAND for a child's linen robe, of woven tapestry, coloured wools and yellow flax on red ground. The pattern, divided into five sections, consists of three panelled arrangements of deteriorated floral and animal forms alternated with a formal leafy branch ornament: the central panel contains two green lions with yellow tails along their backs, vis-à-vis; beyond them on each side are a floral device and a flying (?) youth or cupid. From ancient tombs at Akhmîm (Panopolis), Upper Egypt. ? *Christian Coptic.* ? 6th to 9th cent^y. About 2 ft. 4 in. by 1½ in. Bought (631 to 922, 300*l*.). 779.–1886.

This is noticeable on account of its completeness and the introduction of the flying youth or cupid, appropriate to the band for a child's dress.

BAND (portion of) for a linen robe, of woven tapestry, red wools, and white flax. The pattern consists of three oval panels arranged vertically one above the other

In the upper one is pair of beasts or (?) dragons, with tree between them; in the next are two (front faced) robed men; in the lower one a pair of horses, their heads turned towards one another and a small tree between them. From ancient tombs at Akhmîm (Panopolis), Upper Egypt. ? *Christian Coptic.* ? 6th to 9th centy. About 17½ in. by 4½ in. Bought (631 to 922, 300*l.*). 861.–1886.

No. 860.–1886 is evidently part of the same band. The arrangement of birds, animals, &c. vis-à-vis, in circular medallions is well known in early Assyrian ornament and in Byzantine ornament. See, for instance, the woven band of white and red silk No. 8566.–'63 and No. 8277.–'63 of white and red flax in textile Collections.

BAND (portion of) for a linen robe, of woven tapestry, red wools, and white flax on flax warps. The pattern consists of two (incomplete) oval panels, one above the other. In the upper one are two (front faced) robed men; in the lower a pair of horses, their heads turned towards one another, and a small tree between them. From ancient tombs at Akhmim (Panopolis), Upper Egypt. ? *Christian Coptic.* 6th to 9th centy. About 14 in. by 5½ in. Bought (631 to 922, 300*l.*). 860.–1886.

No. 861.–1886 is evidently part of the same band. See remarks on it.

BAND and SQUARE PANEL (for a robe with surface of rough towel material), of woven tapestry and needlework, brown wool, and yellow flax. The ornament on the band consists of interlaced stem and vine leaf device, with a cartouche containing ? a tulip or an iris. The square panel is bordered with interlaced stem and vine leaf ornament, within which is a square set with circle containing a mounted horseman and hound. From ancient tombs at Akhmîm (Panopolis), Upper Egypt. ? 3rd to 9th centy. About 2 ft. 3 in. by 8½ in. Bought (631 to 922, 300*l.*). 708.–1886.

See also 745.–1886.

BAND and SQUARE PANEL (part of a linen robe), of woven tapestry, brown wool, and yellow flax. The pattern on the band consists of pointed oval shapes in which are ducks in yellow, on brown discs, alternating with roundels containing blossom devices. The border of the square panel is of similar pattern; in centre of square a yellow roundel, containing a brown naked male figure, walking, with staff in right hand, and ends of scarf

hanging from both shoulders, his left arm uplifted.
From ancient tombs at Akhmîm (Panopolis), Upper
Egypt. ? *Egypto-Roman.* ?1st to 6th cent. About
17 in. by 12½ in. Bought (631 to 922, 300*l.*).

707.–1886.

BAND (for linen robe) of woven tapestry, brown wool, and
yellow flax. The pattern consists of a series of oblong
panels, on which, in brown on yellow ground, are alternate naked and draped human figures and animals. The
upper figure is dancing, a ball between his feet; the
lower one, a female (?), is walking holding a scarf (?) in
her hand. Parts picked out in single threads worked
with the needle. From ancient tombs at Akhmîm (Panopolis), Upper Egypt. ? 1st to 6th cent. About 19 in.
by 5¼ in. Bought (631 to 922, 300*l.*).   782.–1886.

BAND and SMALL SQUARE of woven tapestry, dark blue wool,
and yellow flax, part of a linen robe. The band consists
of a narrow guilloche ornament done in needlework
flanked by two bands of blue leaf devices. The square
has a four roundel device in centre, with a border of
guilloche ornament done in needlework. From ancient
tombs at Akhmîm (Panopolis), Upper Egypt. ? 6th to
9th cent. About 20½ in. by 10½ in. Bought (631 to
922, 300*l.*).   720.–1886.

BAND (portion of) for a linen robe, of woven tapestry and
needlework, brown wools and yellow flax. The pattern
consists of a double interchanged key pattern outlined in
single yellow flax threads. From ancient tombs at
Akhmîm (Panopolis), Upper Egypt. ? 3rd to 9th cent.
About 16½ in. by 8 in. Bought (631 to 922, 300*l.*).

800.–1886.

BAND and SQUARE PANEL for a linen robe, of woven
tapestry and needlework, brown wool, and yellow flax.
The pattern on band consists of alternated triple interlacements and diamond and octagonal shapes; that of the
square is of somewhat similar interlaced ornamentation,
set in a border of waved stem with leaf and berry devices;
both patterns outlined in single yellow threads on brown.
From ancient tombs at Akhmîm (Panopolis), Upper
Egypt. ? 3rd to 9th cent. About 2 ft. 9 in. by 16½ in.
Bought (631 to 922, 300*l.*).   797.–1886.

BAND (for a linen robe), of woven tapestry, brown wool, and yellow flax, with pattern of diamond and small roundel devices, worked with the needle in yellow thread on brown. From ancient tombs at Akhmîm (Panopolis), Upper Egypt. ? 1st to 6th centy. About 2 ft. 4 in. by 4¼ in. Bought (631 to 922, 300l.). 814.-1886.

(See 663.)

FRAGMENT of a BAND (for a linen robe), of woven tapestry, brown wool and yellow flax, with a band—between two rows of trefoil or fleurs de lys devices--of guilloche pattern, worked with the needle in single threads on dark brown; at one end the figure of a bird with red beak and grey and red wing. From ancient tombs at Akhmîm (Panopolis), Upper Egypt. ? 3rd to 6th centy. About 6 in. by 3½ in. Bought (631 to 922, 300l.). 905.-1886.

BAND (for a linen robe), of woven tapestry, dark brown, and yellow flax, with fret pattern, worked with the needle in single yellow threads, black; edged on each side with a row of vine leaves. From ancient tombs at Akhmîm (Panopolis), Upper Egypt. ? 1st to 6th centy. About 15½ in. by 3 in. Bought (631 to 922, 300l.).

874.-1886.

BAND (for a linen robe), of woven tapestry, brown wool, and yellow flax, with pattern of diamond and small roundel devices, worked with needle in yellow thread on brown. From ancient tombs at Akhmîm (Panopolis), Upper Egypt. ? 1st to 6th centy. About 2 ft. 2 in. by 4½ in. Bought (631 to 922, 300l.). 663.-1886.

BAND (for a linen robe), of woven tapestry, purple wool, and yellow flax, with a pattern of waved vine stem and leaf device. From ancient tombs at Akhmîm (Panopolis), Upper Egypt. ? 3rd to 9th centy. About 3 ft. 1 in. by 3½ in. Bought (631 to 922, 300l.). 679.-1886.

BAND (for a linen robe), of woven tapestry and needlework, dark brown wool, and yellow flax, with key or fret pattern, worked with the needle in yellow thread on dark brown. From ancient tombs at Akhmîm (Panopolis), Upper Egypt. ? 1st to 6th centy. About 16½ in. by 4 in. Bought (631 to 922, 300l.). 816.-1886.

BAND (for a linen robe), of woven tapestry, dark brown wool, and yellow flax, with key or fret pattern, and occasional rosettes, worked with the needle in yellow thread on dark brown, and edged on both sides with a row of vine leaves. From ancient tombs at Akhmîm (Panopolis), Upper Egypt. ? 1st to 6th cent^y. About 2 ft. 2¾ in. by 3¼ in. Bought (631 to 922, 300*l.*).

813.–1886.

BAND (portion of) for linen robe, of woven tapestry, coloured wools on flax warps. The pattern consists of a series of episodes depicted with figures of men, women, and children, of which the principal are (?) the Virgin (with nimbus) and Christ or a late type of Isis holding (?) a *flabellum* in one hand and a lotus in the other, and Horus.* An upper group of three figures appears to represent Christ making the blind to see; a lower one the raising of widow's son, and lower still are groups which seem to represent a procession. The edging round these groups is of the bud device (see 777.–1886), set between two narrow bands of twisted stems and small leaf patterns. From ancient tombs at Akhmîm (Panopolis), Upper Egypt. *Christian Coptic.* ? 6th to 9th cent^y. About 21 in. by 4 in. (Bought (631 to 922, 300*l.*). 734.–1886.

* The pose of this group is suggestive of that to be seen in allegorical figures of Rome and Constantinople, carved in ivory diptych leaves, such as Nos. 96 and 97.–1866 in the Collection of Ivories.

BAND (portion of) for a linen robe, of woven tapestry, coloured wools on flax warps (much decayed). The central space, bordered with a pattern of floriated device, counterchanged and repeated, contains indications of a saint with nimbus, and various outlined floral ornaments, a tree surmounted by (?) lotus blossoms symmetrically arranged below; all on a red ground. The letters E and � are repeated in various parts. From ancient tombs at Akhmîm (Panopolis), Upper Egypt. *Christian Coptic.* ? 6th to 9th cent^y. About 18¾ in. by 5¼ in. Bought (631 to 922, 300*l.*). 869–1886.

BAND (portion of) for a linen robe, of woven tapestry, coloured wools on flax warp. The pattern consists of three rectangular panels; the upper and lower ones of blue ground, over which are scattered archaic birds and fishes*; the centre panel of red ground, with two standing figures, male and female, the male resting his right arm on a pillar; a blue cloak is thrown over his right arm. His left hand holds a stick. Near the figures is an inscription in Greek characters.

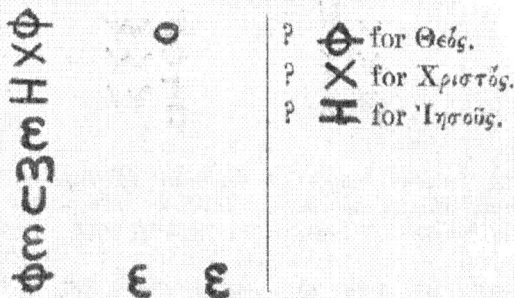

? ⊕ for Θεός.
? ✕ for Χριστός.
? ⊥ for Ἰησοῦς.

From ancient tombs at Akhmîm (Panopolis), Upper Egypt. ?*Egypto-Roman*. ? 3rd to 9th centy. About 13¼ in. by 8¼ in. Bought (631 to 922, 300*l*.).

922.–1886.

* The scattering of birds and beasts and fishes on the ground of a panel shape may be noticed in Roman Mosaics. See Wollaston Collection of Drawings of Mosaics in South Kensington Museum.

BAND (round end, with oval shape pendant, containing bust probably of a saint), of woven tapestry in coloured wools, from a linen robe. This band has a narrow double border of check pattern, between which, on a red ground, are figures of saints (?), the upper one walking, the lower one with his legs (?) in a tomb, and uplifted hands.† From ancient tombs at Akhmîm (Panopolis), Upper Egypt. *Christian Coptic*. ? 6th to 9th centy. About 21½ in. by 4½ in. Bought (631 to 922, 300*l*.). 732.–1886.

† Perhaps typifying the Resurrection in the same sort of primitive style as that of scratched slabs from the Catacombs at Rome representing Noah and the Ark. Along the check borders are occasional yellow panels with red crosses.

BAND (fragment of), formerly of woven tapestry, the coloured wools have been eaten away, the flax warps and parts of the flax weft remain. On the centre of band are figures, of which two are repetitions of a saint standing; at his left foot a little domed building; and (?) of a female saint. The standing figure is placed between two vertical series of Greek characters

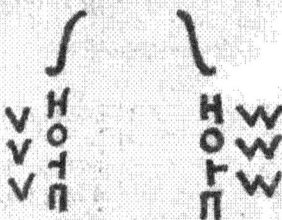

From ancient tombs at Akhmîm (Panopolis), Upper Egypt. *Christian Coptic.* ? 6th to 9th centy. About 18 in. by 4½ in. Bought (631 to 922, 300*l*.). 829.–1886.

BAND with round end and pendant (for a robe), of woven tapestry, coloured wools, and white flax (parts eaten away). Round the edges of the band is a waved stem and leaf ornament. Upon the central ground, red, is a figure of a saint (? St. Paul of Thebes); below him is an ass, upon whose back is a formal triple branched tree (? the sacred Persea), and apparently a bird (? St. Paul's raven), on the haunches of the ass; below comes the tree device and the ass reversed. Within the oval pendant is an animal. From ancient tombs at Akhmîm (Panopolis), Upper Egypt. *Christian Coptic.* ? 6th to 9th centy. About 20 in. by 8½ in. Bought (631 to 922, 300*l*.). 863.–1886.

"Another superstition, which, by this time (early 5th century) the " Pagans had engrafted on Christianity, was that of having sacred trees. " Though the Egyptian Christians had no sacred animals, yet they had " made a tree called the Persea, sacred to Jesus. There was a Persea, " or peach tree, at Hermopolis, which was said to heal the diseases of all " who touched it." (See History of Egypt. S. Sharpe. Vol. II. p. 309. Edward Moxon. London, 1859).

BAND with rounded end for a linen robe, of woven tapestry, of red ground and coloured wools. A rudely drawn waved stem with small floriations runs along the edge of the band. At upper end is part of the figure of a horseman; below is an ass browsing, and two female figures; in the lower part is a saint, with nimbus, ? St. Demetrius on horseback. He carries a staff, with trefoil at top, in his right hand; in his left a sword; a Maltese cross is worked in yellow on his green tunic. Below his horse is a triple leaf branch (? the Persea). From

ancient tombs at Akhmîm (Panopolis), Upper Egypt.
Christian Coptic. ? 6th to 9th cent^y. About 9¼ in. by
4¼ in. Bought (631 to 922, 300*l*.). 739 and 740.–1886.

See also 863.–1886.

BAND (round ended), in very fragmentary condition, formerly of woven tapestry, with coloured wools. The
design was similar in many respects to that of No. 863.–
1886. The indications of animal and leaf forms are comparatively good in drawing. From ancient tombs at
Akhmîm (Panopolis), Upper Egypt. *? Christian Coptic.*
? 6th to 9th cent^y. About 12 in. by 4½ in. Bought (631
to 922, 300*l*.). 847.–1886.

BAND (portion of) for a linen robe, of woven tapestry,
coloured wools. The pattern* consists of a vertical
series of oval panels, in which are deteriorated renderings
of human figures, (?) a man seizing by the head a green
bodied chimera. From ancient tombs at Akhmîm
(Panopolis), Upper Egypt. *? Christian Coptic.* ? 6th to
9th cent^y. About 15½ in. by 4¾ in. Bought (631 t
922, 300*l*.). 851.–1886.

* The arrangement here is similar to that of pattern in Nos. 860 and 861.–
1886 ; see remarks on latter. The edging to this band consists of repeated
and reversed small stiff trefoil sprays. The figures are outlined with black.

BAND (portion of) for a linen robe, of woven tapestry,
coloured wools. The pattern consists of a centre band,
red ground, with repeated oval forms, containing deteriorated representations of birds and other emblems ;
between the oval forms are red crosses. On each side
of the centre is a rude scroll ornament ; the scrolls
terminated in (?) bird heads. From ancient tombs
at Akhmîm (Panopolis), Upper Egypt. *Christian Coptic.*
? 6th to 9th cent^y. About 3 ft. 1 in. by 5¼ in. Bought
(631 to 922, 300*l*.). 781.–1886.

BAND (portion of) for a linen robe, of linen, with two stripes,
and symmetrically arranged devices, worked in tapestry
weaving with coloured wools. The stripes are ornamented
with a thin continuous waved stem pattern of yellow
flax with brown wool ; on the linen ground between them
are various pear-shaped (? tree) forms, placed at even
distances one above the other ; between them are pairs of

?rose buds.* From ancient tombs at Akhmím (Panopolis),
Upper Egypt. ? 6th to 9th cent?. About 2 ft. by 4 in.
Bought (631 to 922, 300*l.*). 777.-1886

* See similar devices and colours in Robe No. 634.-1886 ; also in the
narrow bands of Byzantine woven silk specimen No. 7036.-1860 ; and in the
latus clavus of the attendant to the left of the Empress Theodora in the
Mosaic at Church of San Vitale, Ravenna (A.D. 547). See also similar
scheme of ornament in No. 646.-1886.

BAND (portion of) for a linen robe, of woven tapestry, of red
ground, and coloured wools, with a representation of a man
blowing a horn shaped like a Byzantine ivory oliphant, and
seated in a high-backed chariot drawn by grotesque horse
or camel ; below him are two men, walking ; the one on
the left carrying (?) a basket or quiver on his back ; the
one on the right carrying a (?) disc. From ancient tombs
at Akhmím (Panopolis), Upper Egypt. *Christian Coptic.*
? 6th to 9th cent?. About 8½ in. by 4½ in. Bought (631
to 922, 300*l.*). 737.-1886.

The figures are outlined in black, see also 737*a*.-1886.

BAND (portion of) for a linen robe, of woven tapestry, of
faded red ground, and coloured wools, with a representation of a man blowing a horn shaped like a Byzantine
ivory oliphant), seated in a high-backed chariot drawn by
grotesque horse or camel ; below him are two men,
walking ; the one on the left carrying (?) a basket or
quiver on his back ; the one on the right carrying a (?) disc.
The wools in upper part of the base are eaten away.
From ancient tombs at Akhmím (Panopolis), Upper
Egypt. *Christian Coptic.* ? 3rd to 9th cent?. About
10 in. by   in. Bought (631 to 922, 300*l.*).

737*a*.-1886.

The figures are outlined in black, see also 737.-1886.

BAND (part of), of woven tapestry, coloured wools, and
yellow flax, from a linen robe. The outer edges have
green bands with yellow scroll ornament ; the central
band of red ground has three panels, the upper and
lower of which are filled with repeating diamond and
scroll pattern ; in the panel between them is the
figure of walking saint (?) carrying a bird, with a red
claw, on his left arm (? St. Paul of Thebes) ; above him
(?) a winged angel. From ancient tombs at Akhmím
(Panopolis), Upper Egypt. *Christian Coptic.* ? 6th to
9th cent?. About 13? in. by 3½ in. Bought (631 to
922, 300*l.*). 849.-1886.

BAND (part of) for a robe, of woven tapestry, coloured
wools, with debased renderings of birds and flowers symmetrically arranged one above the other in two vertical
series. At one end there is a circle containing two birds
vis-à-vis, with a tree between them. This marks
where band rested on the shoulder. From ancient tombs
at Akhmîm (Panopolis), Upper Egypt. *Christian Coptic.*
? 6th to 9th centy. About 7 in. by 2¾ in. Bought (631
to 922, 300*l*.).   884.-1886.

BORDER (fragment) of woven tapestry, coloured wools, and
flax, part of a linen robe (?) for ecclesiastical purposes.
The pattern consists of robed figures with *nimbi*
(? priests) holding in right hands, staves terminated with
cones or buds, and in left hands discs, each between
flowering plants, and alternating with white medallions,
filled in with squares, and deteriorated floral forms symmetrically arranged. Between each figure and medallion
is a tree device. From ancient tombs at Akhmîm (Panopolis), Upper Egypt. *Christian Coptic.* ? 6th to 9th
centy. About 3 ft. 2 in. by 4 in. Bought (631 to 922,
300*l*.).   667.-1886.

BAND (rounded end of), with pendant,* for a linen robe,
of woven tapestry, coloured wools and flax. A triple
border of repeated degraded floral and other details
runs round the band, in centre panel of which,
is a figure with green jacket and yellow skirt, arms
uplifted, (? a priest in act of benediction), with sleeves
hanging from elbows. In the panels above and below
her are three sets of grotesque figures, one holding
up (?) a scarf over his head. All the figures are outlined
in black. From ancient tombs at Akhmîm (Panopolis),
Upper Egypt. *Christian Coptic.* ? 6th to 9th centy.
About 23¼ in. by 4 in. Bought (631 to 922, 300*l*.).
                                                       733.-1886.

* The medallion 742.-1886 probably came from the same robe as this
band. The ornament in the pendant is a deteriorated rendering of such an
animal as is seen in the pendant No. 856.-1886.

BAND (portion of) for a linen robe, of woven tapestry,
coloured wools. The pattern consists of alternate
panellings of red and yellow ground. On the red
ground panel is a figure of a woman with nimbus (see
734-1886) seated. On the yellow grounds the details
are of deteriorated floral and nondescript forms. This
main band is edged with rude yellow scroll ornament on

                                                       B 2

narrow black ground. From ancient tombs at Akhmîm (Panopolis), Upper Egypt. *Christian Coptic.* ? 6th to 9th cent^y. About 18 in. by 2½ in. Bought (631 to 922, 300*l.*). 736.-1883.

BAND (portion of, round ended,) for a linen robe, of woven tapestry, coloured wools. The pattern consists of rude forms symmetrically arranged, to form a pair of objects, one on each side of a budding plant, and the two objects together, flanked by the budding plant. The pattern on edge is a series of detached double scroll forms. From ancient tombs at Akhmîm (Panopolis), Upper Egypt. *Christian Coptic?* ? 6th to 9th cent^y. About 13½ in. by 3½ in. Bought (631 to 922, 300*l.*).
870.-1886.

The arrangement here suggests a survival of the well known Assyrian device of two confronted animals or birds with a tree between them.

BAND (portion of) for a linen robe, of woven tapestry, coloured wools and flax. The pattern consists of two panels with red ground, in one is figured a nude man climbing a tree to escape from a long necked camel; and in the other a man with uplifted hands standing near an open-mouthed beast. The edging on each side of the panels is a continuous waved and pleated stem in yellow on blue. From ancient tombs at Akhmîm (Panopolis), Upper Egypt. *Christian Coptic.* ? 6th to 9th cent^y. About 11 in. by 8¼ in. Bought (631 to 922, 300*l.*).
866.-1886.

BAND (portion of) for a linen robe, of woven tapestry coloured wools, on flax warps (much eaten away). Between two narrow rows of lily devices repeated, a red ground with a figure of a horseman (?) St. George, and beneath him a dragon (?). From ancient tombs at Akhmîm (Panopolis), Upper Egypt. *Christian Coptic.* ? 6th to 9th cent^y. About 10¼ in. by 3½ in. Bought (631 to 922, 300*l.*). 741.-1886.

BAND (end of) for a linen robe, of woven tapestry, coloured wools. The pattern (rudely drawn) consists of a draped female figure with *nimbus* and animals on a crimson ground. From ancient tombs at Akhmîm (Panopolis), Upper Egypt. *Christian Coptic.* ? 6th to 9th cent^y. About 18¼ in. by 2 in. Bought (631 to 922, 300*l.*).
735.-1886.

See also 733.-1886, in which a woman wearing a similar skirt is shown, and 670 in respect of similar rudely drawn animals.

BAND (portion of) for a linen robe, of woven tapestry, coloured wools.* The pattern consists of vertically repeated groups of deteriorated floral and nondescript forms set between two edges of intertwisting stem ornament. From ancient tombs at Akhmîm (Panopolis), Upper Egypt. ? 6th to 9th centy. About 14½ in. by 7¾ in. Bought (631 to 922, 300*l.*). 771.–1886.

* The colours have well kept their tones. The specimen may date from comparatively recent times.

BAND (round ended) for a robe, of woven tapestry, coloured wools (almost entirely eaten away, so that the flax threads alone remain). From ancient tombs at Akhmîm (Panopolis), Upper Egypt. *Christian Coptic.* ? 6th to 9th centy. About 11¾ in. by 2½ in. Bought (631 to 922, 300*l.*). 827.–1886.

BAND (portion of), round ended, one with pendant (for a robe), of woven tapestry, coloured wools (much decayed). The ornament along the edges is of leaf scroll devices, in yellow flax on green ground. The main ground was red wool, on which were human figures of saints. From ancient tombs at Akhmîm (Panopolis), Upper Egypt. *Christian Coptic.* ? 6th to 9th centy. About 14½ in. by 3¼ in. Bought (631 to 922, 300*l.*). 831.–1886.

BAND (in very fragmentary condition) for a robe, of woven tapestry, coloured wools. The pattern appears to have consisted of oval divisions, in which were human figures and animals. From ancient tombs at Akhmîm (Panopolis), Upper Egypt. *? Christian Coptic.* ? 6th to 9th centy. About 17½ in. by 3½ in. Bought (631 to 922, 300*l.*). 852.–1886.

BAND (in fragmentary condition) for a robe, of woven tapestry, coloured wools, with indications of human figures and formal devices. From ancient tombs at Akhmîm (Panopolis), Upper Egypt. *? Christian Coptic.* ? 6th to 9th centy. About 8¼ in. by 4¼ in. Bought (631 to 922, 300*l.*). 738.–1886.

BAND (in fragmentary condition) for a robe, of woven tapestry, coloured wools, with figures mounted on asses and a female saint, with skirt, on red ground within a double border of small roundels, and a sort of check pattern. From ancient tombs at Akhmim (Panopolis), Upper Egypt. *Christian Coptic.* ? 6th to 9th cent^y. About 8¼ in. by 4½ in. Bought (631 to 922, 300*l*.).

853 and 854–1886.

BANDS (fragments of two) for a linen robe, of woven tapestry, coloured wool, with a vertical series of human figures, and animals between which runs a long tree stem upon red ground, and between two narrow edging bands of small roundel pattern. From ancient tombs at Akhmim (Panopolis), Upper Egypt. *? Christian Coptic.* ? 6th to 9th cent^y. About 2 ft. by 17 in., and 10 in. by 6½ in. Bought (631 to 922, 300*l*.). 848 and 848*a*.–1886.

BAND (round ended with pendant), of woven tapestry (much decayed), coloured wools, with figures mounted on asses and a saint with skirt on red ground within a double border of small roundels, and a sort of check pattern. From ancient tombs at Akhmim (Panopolis), Upper Egypt. *? Christian Coptic.* ? 6th to 9th cent^y. About 20 in. by 3½ in. Bought (631 to 922, 300*l*.).

850.—1886.

See also 853 and 854.–1886.

BAND (rounded end of) for a linen robe, of woven tapestry, coloured wools, two figures mounted on asses within a double border. From ancient tombs at Akhmim (Panopolis), Upper Egypt. *? Christian Coptic.* ? 6th to 9th cent^y. About 7 in. by 4 in. Bought (631 to 922, 300*l*.).

845.–1886.

See also 850, 853, and 854.

BAND (for a child's linen robe), of woven tapestry, coloured wools; with yellow double stem ornament forming a series of small pointed oval shapes, filled in with variously coloured buds (?) on red ground. From ancient tombs at Akhmim (Panopolis), Upper Egypt. ? 6th to 9th cent^y. About 12 in. by 5½ in. Bought (631 to 922, 300*l*.).

882.–1886.

BANDS (part of two, with breast panel between them), for a linen robe, of woven tapestry, with coloured wools. The pattern along the bands consists of long divisions, alternately filled in with (?) dogs and birds on green ground; and balanced fruit stem (? pomegranate or circle with cross device) pattern on red ground, and set between double borders of small repeating ornaments. The breast band

(more than half of which is eaten away) was formerly
ornamented with a procession of four figures, whose
skirts and feet remain. From ancient tombs at Akhmim
(Panopolis), Upper Egypt. ? *Christian Coptic.* ? 6th to
9th centy. About 20 in. by 12 in. Bought (631 to 922,
300*l.*). 871.–1886.

BAND (portion of) for a child's robe, of woven tapestry, red
and blue wools, in alternate groups of heart-shaped leaf
ornament. From ancient tombs at Akhmim (Panopolis),
Upper Egypt. ? 6th to 9th centy. About 23 in. by
2½ in. Bought (631 to 922, 300*l.*). 780.–1886.

BAND (portion of) for a child's linen robe, of woven tapestry,
red and blue wools, in alternate groups of heart-shaped
leaf ornament. From ancient tombs at Akhmim (Panopolis), Upper Egypt. ? 6th to 9th centy. About 10½ in.
by 2½ in. Bought (631 to 922, 300*l.*). 780*a.*–1886.

BAND (portion of) for a linen robe, of woven tapestry, red,
and brown wools and yellow flax. The pattern consists
of two intertwisting stems forming a series of circular
panels, in each of which are figures representing alternately (?) a man seizing another by the hair of the head,
and (?) a fight between a lion and a man. From ancient
tombs at Akhmim (Panopolis), Upper Egypt. ? 6th to
9th centy. 16¼ in. by 6 in. Bought (631 to 922, 300*l.*).
772.–1886.

The forms are very deteriorated in the rendering. See also 851.–1886.

BAND (portion of) for a linen cloth (?), of woven tapestry
(coloured wools eaten away). The pattern* consists of
narrow bands arranged to cross one another. In the
spaces between them are rosette ornaments. From
ancient tombs at Akhmim (Panopolis), Upper Egypt.
? 6th to 9th centy. About 13 in. by 6 in. Bought (631
to 922, 300*l.*). 826.–1886.

* See similar pattern in No. 896.–1886, and No. 888.–1886.

BAND (portion of) for a linen cloth (?), of woven tapestry,
red, green, and white wools. The pattern consists of
narrow bands to form trellis divisions, within which are
floriated cross devices. From ancient tombs at Akhmim
(Panopolis), Upper Egypt. ? 6th to 9th centy. About
12 in. by 6½ in. Bought (631 to 922, 300*l.*). 896.–1886.

Compare with pattern in No. 826 and No. 888.–1886 This is also
suggestive of the 15th century white linen and red silk embroidery
patterns of the Italians and Greeks. See 146.–'80, and 586.–'84, white
and black specimen from the Abruzzi in the South Kensington Museum.

BAND (portion of broad) (?) for a linen cloth, of woven tapestry, red and white wools on flax warps. The pattern consists of narrow bands of key pattern, filled in with ovals, Maltese crosses, and (?) fleurs de lys, and arranged to form trellis divisions, within which are ornamental crosses set within hexagonal grounds, about which are eight pointed star shapes. From ancient tombs at Akhmîm (Panopolis), Upper Egypt. ? 6th to 9th cent^y. About 10½ in. by 8¼ in. Bought (631 to 922, 300*l.*) 888.–1886.

BAND (portion of) for a linen robe, of woven tapestry, brown and yellow wools. The pattern consists of a series of circular panels with animals and trees alternately.* From ancient tombs at Akhmîm (Panopolis), Upper Egypt. *? Egypto-Byzantine.* 6th to 9th cent^y. About 21 in. by 5½ in. Bought (631 to 922, 300*l.*). 659.–1886.

* See also 660.–1886, of more refined design and lighter texture.

BAND (portion of) for a linen robe, of woven tapestry, brown and yellow wools. The pattern consists of a series of oblong and square panels alternated. In the former are rudely drawn, costumed and naked, standing figures; in the latter, rudely drawn animals. From ancient tombs at Akhmîm (Panopolis), Upper Egypt. ? 6th to 9th cent^y. About 2 ft. 1½ in. by 3¼ in. Bought (631 to 922, 300*l.*). 785.–1886.

The drawing of the pattern is very rude, and somewhat similar to that in such specimens as No. 787–1886, and is possibly of a later date.

BAND (end of narrow) for a linen robe, of woven tapestry, purple wool and yellow flax. The pattern consists of a waved stem, with foliage and a bird placed in every third wave. From ancient tombs at Akhmîm (Panopolis), Upper Egypt. ? 3rd to 6th cent^y. About 20½ in. by 2½ in. Bought (631 to 922, 300*l.*). 677.–1886.

BAND (end of) for a linen robe, of woven tapestry, purple wool and yellow flax. The pattern consists of a thick waved stem with two leaves of ornamental character in each wave. From ancient tombs at Akhmîm (Panopolis), Upper Egypt. *Egypto-Roman.* ? 3rd to 6th cent^y. About 16¾ in. by 4 in. Bought (631 to 922, 300*l.*). 793.–1886.

BAND (portion of) for a linen robe, of woven tapestry, brown and yellow wools. The pattern consists of a central brown band with repeated bud or heart devices worked with the needle in outline, flanked by (?) vine leaf devices, repeated to form a border. From ancient tombs at Akhmîm (Panopolis), Upper Egypt. 6th to 9th centy. About 11½ in. by 4½ in. Bought (631 to 922, 300*l.*).

908.-1886.

See coloured bud ornament in 777.-1886.

BAND (narrow) from a linen robe, of woven tapestry, brown wool and yellow flax with a foliated scroll ornament down centre of it. From ancient tombs at Akhmîm (Panopolis), Upper Egypt. *Egypto-Byzantine.* ? 6th to 9th centy. About 7¼ in. by 4½ in. Bought (631 to 922, 300*l.*).

918.-1886.

BAND (end of narrow) for a linen robe, of woven tapestry, dark blue wool and yellow flax. The pattern consists of double branched devices, alternated with a version of the outstretched figure in No. 721.-1886, and set between two borders of wave lined and spot ornament. From ancient tombs at Akhmîm (Panopolis), Upper Egypt. ? 6th to 9th centy. *Christian Coptic.* About 21½ in. by 4½ in. Bought (631 to 922, 300*l.*).

868.-1886.

BAND (portion of) for linen robe, of woven tapestry, brown wool and yellow flax. The pattern consists of linked quatrefoils divisions ; within each is a four-leaf device. This arrangement is set between two small scalloped edges. From ancient tombs at Akhmîm (Panopolis), Upper Egypt. *Egypto-Byzantine.* ? 6th to 9th centy. About 3 ft. 1 in. by 2¾ in. Bought (631 to 922, 300*l.*).

673.-1886.

BAND (portion of) for a linen robe, of woven tapestry brown wool and yellow flax. The pattern consists of a vertical series of two handled flower vases, between scalloped borders of vine leaves. From ancient tombs at Akhmîm (Panopolis), Upper Egypt. ? 6th to 9th centy. About 3 ft. 5 in. by 4 in. Bought (631 to 922, 300*l.*).

647.-1886.

Compare also with 913.-1886. The vases there are of more classic shapes than those here, which are of a Persian type.

BAND (portion of) for a linen robe, of woven tapestry,
dark blue wool and white flax; a guilloche pattern,
worked with the needle in single threads on blue ground,
is set between two borders of intertwisting stems; in the
panels thus formed are four crosses of leaf devices. A
yellow cross device is set in a blue ground in the centre
of guilloche pattern. From ancient tombs at Akhmîm
(Panopolis), Upper Egypt. ? 6th to 9th centʸ. ? *Egypto-
Byzantine.* About 17¼ in. by 3 in. Bought (631 to
922, 300*l.*).   912.–1886.

BAND (double-portion of) for a linen robe, of woven
tapestry and needlework, brown wool and yellow flax.
The pattern* in each band consists of a waved stem,
with (?) a leaf device set in each wave, and is outlined in
single threads on brown. From ancient tombs at Akhmîm
(Panopolis), Upper Egypt. ?6th to 9th centʸ. About
3 ft. by 3¼ in. Bought (631 to 922, 300*l.*). 792.–1886.

* This pattern and its general appearance recall embroidery on pashmena
done in Cashmere.

BAND (end of) for a linen robe, of woven tapestry and
needlework, brown wool and yellow flax. The pattern,
outlined in single threads on a brown ground, consists of
two, short, close-lying stems, with twisted ends, in repeated
groups. From ancient tombs at Akhmim (Panopolis),
Upper Egypt. 6th to 9th centʸ. About 12 in. by 5¾
in. Bought (631 to 922, 300*l.*).   907.–1886.

BAND (double-portion of) for a linen robe, of woven tapestry, brown wool and yellow flax. The pattern consists
of four-leaf devices alternated with pointed ovals. In one
band the pointed ovals contain a white centre and brown
cross, in the other a four-leaf device, worked with the
needle in thread on the brown ground. Both bands are
edged with the wave pattern. From ancient tombs at
Akhmîm (Panopolis), Upper Egypt. ? 6th to 9th centʸ.
About 17 in. by 10½ in. Bought (631 to 922, 300*l.*).
                                                687.–1886.

BANDS (two, parts of) for a linen robe, of woven tapestry,
brown wool and yellow flax, with twisted stem ornament and leaf devices in open pointed oval spaces. From
ancient tombs at Akhmim (Panopolis), Upper Egypt.
?6th to 9th centʸ. About 17 in. by 11 in. Bought (631
to 922, 300*l.*).   665.–1886.

BANDS (two, parts of) for a linen robe, of woven tapestry, black wool and yellow flax, with repeated vine leaf and tendril device. From ancient tombs at Akhmîm (Panopolis), Upper Egypt. ? 6th to 9th centy. About 2 ft. 2½ in. by 5½ in. Bought (631 to 922, 300*l*.)

683.–1886.

BANDS (two, parts of), with large medallion, for a linen robe or cloth, of woven tapestry and needlework, brown wool and yellow flax. In centre of medallion is an octagonal space, filled with interlacing scroll ornament. About the octagon are two interlacing bands with rude wave pattern forming squares outside alternate sides of the octagon. This group is inclosed in circular band of double scroll devices, arranged closely to one another; all outlined in needlework of single yellow threads upon brown. The bands are of brown waved stem and berry ornament, with a grotesque bird at one point pecking at these berries. From ancient tombs at Akhmîm (Panopolis), Upper Egypt. ? 6th to 9th centy. About 2 ft. 5½ in. by 2 ft. 2 in. Bought (631 to 922, 300*l*.). 726.–1886.

" Birds eating grapes occur in one or two wood carvings." (Ancient Coptic Churches. Butler, vol. ii. p. 92). A comparison may also be made between bands of closely arranged details in this specimen and the narrow bands of carved ornament on the 6th century ivory chair of St. Maximian at Ravenna. The scheme of ornament in the medallion survives in the Arab brass plateaux or trays engraved and beaten similarly at the present day in Morocco.

BAND (for neck of a linen robe), of woven tapestry, brown wool and yellow flax, showing an ornamented trellis pattern, with combined square and quatrefoil devices, filled in with cross and symmetrically arranged trefoil forms. From ancient tombs at Akhmim (Panopolis), Upper Egypt. ? 6th to 9th centy. About 2 ft. 4 in. by 8 in. Bought (631 to 922, 300*l*.). 729.—1886.

The button at opening about neck remains on this band. The band hung down the centre of the robe, back and front, and opens into a sort of collar round the neck.

BAND (fragment of) for a linen robe, of woven tapestry, red and black wools. The pattern consists of repeated black squares with red roundels set in them, on the roundels are small diamond and scroll motives symmetrically grouped. From ancient tombs at Akhmîm (Panopolis), Upper Egypt. ? 6th to 9th centy. About 10¾ in. by 5¼ in. Bought (631 to 922, 300*l*.). 887.–1886.

BAND (fragment of) for a linen robe, of woven tapestry, red and black wools, with diaper ornament of waved ivy stems about diamond forms. From ancient tombs at Akhmîm (Panopolis), Upper Egypt. ? 6th to 9th centy. About 9½ in. by 2¼ in. Bought (631 to 922, 300*l.*).
886.-1886.

BAND (fragment), of woven tapestry, brown and orange wool; the patterns of two sizes of waved stem and leaf ornament. From ancient tombs at Akhmîm (Panopolis), Upper Egypt. ? 6th to 9th centy. About 6½ in. by 4 in. Bought (631 to 922, 300*l.*).
890.-1886.

BAND (narrow) and small MEDALLION, from a linen robe, of woven tapestry, brown wool and yellow flax. The small band consists of panels of scroll pattern, alternated with foliated scrolls and with panels on which are small yellow discs; the band terminates in a narrow stem with trefoil. The medallion (part only preserved) has a centre roundel, on which is an interlaced stem pattern worked with the needle; the border about it is of foliated scrolls. Beyond the medallion is the tree device, flanked by two fanciful birds.* From ancient tombs at Akhmîm (Panopolis), Upper Egypt. ? 7th to 9th centy. *? Egypto-Byzantine.* About 17 in. by 5 in. Bought (631 to 922, 300*l.*).
675.-1886.

* This additional ornamentation to the medallion marks a further fashion in this class of ornaments, and must therefore be of comparatively late date, say, from 7th to 9th century.

BAND (end of) for a linen robe, of woven tapestry and needlework, dark blue wool and yellow flax. The pattern of a repeated key motive, picked out in single threads of yellow, is set between two edgings of (?) vine leaf devices. From ancient tombs at Akhmîm (Panopolis), Upper Egypt. ? 6th to 9th centy. About 2 ft. 1 in. by 3¼ in. Bought (631 to 922, 300*l.*).
662.-1886.

See also 664.-1886.

BAND (portion of) for a linen robe, of woven tapestry and needlework, brown and yellow flax. The centre is filled with a repeated key pattern, with rosettes in some of the spaces; all outlined in yellow threads on brown ground, and set between two edgings of (?) vine leaf scallops. From ancient tombs at Akhmîm (Panopolis), Upper Egypt. ? 6th to 9th centy. About 2 ft. 3 in. by 4 in. Bought (631 to 922, 300*l.*).
664.-1886.

See also 800.-1886.

BANDS (triple, ends of) for a linen robe, of woven tapestry,
coloured wools. The central and broader band contains
a repeated stem blossom and leaf ornament, on yellow
ground ; the narrower bands, one on each side of it, are
of dark brown and dark green, chevron pattern, with
occasional yellow and red roundels upon them. From
ancient tombs at Akhmim (Panopolis), Upper Egypt.
? 9th centy. About 20¼ in. by 9¼ in. Bought (631 to
922, 300*l*.). 761.–1886.

This specimen is the only one of its kind. The freshness of the
colours and intact quality of the work suggest a comparatively recent
origin for it.

BAND (part of) for skirt of a loosely-woven yellow flax robe,
with insertions of woven tapestry in coloured wools, consisting of detached leaves and fruit forms ; in one of them
is a green bird on white ground. From ancient tombs at
Akhmîm (Panopolis), Upper Egypt. ? 6th to 9th century.
About 2 ft. 1 in. by 7 in. Bought (631 to 922, 300*l*.).
646.–1886.

See similar scheme of ornament in No. 777.–1866.

BAND (part of) for a linen robe, of woven tapestry, coloured
wools. The pattern (rude in character) consists of a
waved stem with leaf devices. From ancient tombs at
Akhmîm (Panopolis), Upper Egypt. ? 6th to 9th centy.
About 11 in. by 2 in. Bought (631 to 922, 300*l*.).
885.–1886.

(c.) HOOD.

HOOD, of rough towel material, faced on one side with flax
loops, (see note to 709.–1866) with two bands, formerly
of woven tapestry, with coloured wools, now almost
entirely eaten away. From ancient tombs at Akhmîm
(Panopolis), Upper Egypt. ? 6th to 9th centy. About
19 in. by 15 in. Bought 631 to 922, 300*l*.). 839.–1886.

(*d.*) CUFFS and SLEEVES for robes chiefly of the tunic shape.

CUFF (two broad bands for), of woven tapestry, brown wool, and yellow flax, from a linen robe. Each band is ornamented with a vertical series of four roundels, in which are alternately figured, formal tree and leaf device, and grotesque nude human figures, one bearing a staff in each hand, and one a basket of fruit. From ancient tombs at Akhmîm (Panopolis), Upper Egypt. ? 3rd to 9th cent*y*. About 14½ in. by 14 in. Bought (631 to 922, 300*l*.).

791.–1886.

CUFF (two bands for), of woven tapestry, brown wool, and yellow flax, from a linen robe. Each band is ornamented with three linked roundels, in which are alternately figured, animals, (?) dog and hare, and a naked human figure, with floral branch in each hand (one up, the other down), and a scarf hanging from right arm. From ancient tombs at Akhmîm (Panopolis), Upper Egypt. ? 1st to 6th cent*y*. About 11½ in. by 6 in. Bought (631 to 922, 300*l*.).

809.–1886.

CUFF (two broad bands for), of woven tapestry, dark blue and yellow wools, from a linen robe. The bands were divided into panels (of which three remain), in which are clumsily proportioned naked male figures, with waist band and apron, among vine stems, leaves, and grapes. From ancient tombs at Akhmîm (Panopolis), Upper Egypt. ? 3rd to 9th cent*y*. About 10 in. by 5½ in. Bought (631 to 922, 300*l*.).

787.–1886.

CUFF (two narrow bands for), of woven tapestry and needlework, brown wool and yellow flax, from a rough towel-faced robe. Each band consists of alternations of sea monsters, set in panels of yellow ground, and diapered panels, with varied diamond ornament, in yellow on brown. From ancient tombs at Akhmîm (Panopolis), Upper Egypt. ? *Egypto-Roman.* ? 3rd to 6th cent*y*. About 12 in. by 5 in. Bought (631 to 922, 300*l*.).

717.–1886.

CUFF (two narrow bands for), of woven tapestry, brown wool, and yellow flax, from a linen robe. The bands consist of a waved stem, with ornamental leaves in each

wave. From ancient tombs at Akhmîm (Panopolis),
Upper Egypt. ?3rd to 9th centy. About 14 in. by 8 in.
Bought (631 to 922, 300l.).   686.-1886.

CUFF (two narrow bands for), of woven tapestry, dark blue
wool and yellow flax, from a linen robe. The pattern
consists of a vertical series of two scroll-handled amphora
shaped vases with formal leaf sprays, blue on yellow.
From ancient tombs at Akhmîm (Panopolis), Upper
Egypt. ? Egypto-Roman. ? 1st to 6th centy. About
10½ in. by 3½ in. Bought (631 to 922, 300l.).
                                                 648.-1886.

This is probably from the same robe as that from which the band
No. 834.-1886 was taken.

CUFF (two narrow bands for), of woven tapestry, brown
wools, and yellow flax, from a linen robe. The pattern
consists of a waved stem, with ivy leaves on each side of
it. From ancient tombs at Akhmîm (Panopolis), Upper
Egypt. ? Egypto-Roman. ? 1st to 6th centy. About
11½ in. by 6 in. Bought (631 to 922, 300l.). 681.-1886.

This is probably from the same robe as that from which the band
No. 706.-1886 was taken.

CUFF (two bands for), of woven tapestry, dark blue wool,
and yellow flax, from a linen robe. In centre of each band
is a guilloche and zigzag pattern, flanked on each side
by a narrow band of small roundels and square vine leaf
devices; between the two bands is a waved stem with
ivy leaves. The ornament is outlined in needlework
with yellow flax. From ancient tombs at Akhmîm
(Panopolis), Upper Egypt. ?1st to 6th centy. About
11¼ in. by 7 in. Bought (631 to 922, 300l.). 718.-1886.

CUFF (two broad bands for), of woven tapestry, brown
wool, and yellow flax, from a linen robe. The bands are
wider than usual, and have an edging of tassel ornament,
between which is a waved vine leaf stem; the fibres of
which are done in needlework. From ancient tombs at
Akhmîm (Panopolis), Upper Egypt. ? Egypto-Roman.
?3rd to 6th centy. About 14 in. by 6¾ in. Bought
(631 to 922, 300l.).   676.-1886.

CUFF (two narrow bands for), of woven tapestry, brown
wool, and yellow flax, from a towel-faced linen robe.
Each band consists of groups of two vine stems with
leaves, intertwisted, with circular panels inserted at equal

distances; upon the brown circular panels are six petalled
figures, in centre of which is a small vine leaf. From
ancient tombs at Akhmîm (Panopolis), Upper Egypt.
Egypto-Byzantine. ? 3rd to 9th centy. About 15 in. by
4½ in. Bought (631 to 922, 300*l.*). 682.-1886.

Cuff, of woven tapestry, red wool, and white flax, from a
linen robe. The broader part of the cuff consists of an
oblong, with a central vertical panel containing a roundel,
in which is a man's head, with hand holding a blossomed
stem; on each side of the vertical panel are two horizontal panels, each containing two roundels, upon which
are rude figures of birds. The top and bottom of the
oblong are bordered with repeated ornament in outline,
(?) fruits and leaves. The small ornament by the wrist
is a fragment upon which two grotesque animals *vis à vis*
appear. From ancient tombs at Akhmîm (Panopolis),
Upper Egypt. ? *Christian Coptic.* ? 6th to 9th centy.
About 10½ in. by 8½ in. Bought (631 to 922, 300*l.*).

723.-1886.

This red and white work is similar to that of No. 832.-1886. The
button and loop on this cuff are intact.

Cuff (part of), of woven tapestry, coloured wools, from a
linen robe. The oblong contains a vertical band with
roundel, in which is the bust of a saint (?) with *nimbus*,
between two dog-headed anubi. On each side of the
vertical panel are two horizontal panels with figures
(one of which is reversed) of horsemen (one side of this
piece is eaten away). From ancient tombs at Akhmîm
(Panopolis), Upper Egypt. *Christian Coptic.* ? 6th to
9th centy. About 11 in. by 6 in. Bought (631 to 922,
300*l.*). 864.-1886.

Cuff (two bands for), of woven tapestry, brown wool, and
yellow flax, from a linen robe. Each band is edged with
small scallop shapes, between which is a series of eight
yellow roundels, with leaf device in brown upon one
series, and alternate (?) ducks and leaf devices upon the
other. From ancient tombs at Akhmîm (Panopolis),
Upper Egypt. ? 6th to 9th centy. About 12 in. by
7 in. Bought (631 to 922, 300*l.*). 685.-1886.

Cuff (two bands for), of woven tapestry, dark blue and
brown flax. The bands are wider than usual and consist
of a double stem scroll ornament, with leaves in the

spaces between the stems in black wool. From ancient tombs at Akhmim (Panopolis), Upper Egypt. ? 6th to 9th centy. *Egypto-Byzantine.* About 11 in. by 10½ in. Bought (631 to 922, 300*l.*). 917.–1886.

CUFF with SQUARE PANEL, of woven tapestry, coloured wools, and flax. In centre a star device, filled in with debased floral ornaments; around this a diamond framework, with roundels and blossoms inserted at the angles ; portions of star form are repeated in outer corners. From ancient tombs at Akhmîm (Panopolis), Upper Egypt. ? *Christian Coptic.* ? 6th to 9th centy. About 17 in. by 14¼ in. Bought (631 to 922, 300*l.*).
889.–1886.

CUFF (two narrow bands for), of woven tapestry, dark blue wool, and yellow flax, from a linen robe. Each band consists of alternations of scrolls in blue on yellow, and scrolls set within a panel, the ground of which is worked over with the needle in yellow threads. From ancient tombs at Akhmim (Panopolis), Upper Egypt. ?3rd to 9th centy. About 11½ in. by 3¾ in. Bought (631 to 922, 300*l.*). 684.–1886.

CUFF (part of) for a linen robe, of woven tapestry, coloured wools, with broad band containing two panels of grey, red, and orange, upon which are arranged formal floral ornaments set in irregular hexagon shapes. From ancient tombs at Akhmim (Panopolis), Upper Egypt. ? 6th to 9th centy. About 9 in. by 6½ in. Bought (631 to 922, 300*l.*). 778.–1886.

(e.) SQUARE PANELS (*tabulæ*) for shoulders and skirts of robes chiefly of the tunic class.

SQUARE PANEL, of woven tapestry, in variously coloured wools of fine thread, for a robe. Within a scarlet frame, upon which is a floral ornament, is a representation, upon a dark purple ground, of a demi-figure of Hermes holding the caduceus in one hand and a purse in the other. About his head is a *nimbus.* His name is indicated in Greek characters, E P M H°. From ancient tombs at

Akhmîm (Panopolis), Upper Egypt. *Egypto-Roman.* ? 1st to 4th cent^y A.D. 6½ in. square. Bought (631 to 922, 300*l.*). 651.–1886.

The style of this panel recalls Pompeian and other Roman decoration of the 1st century B.C. and A.D. See also 652 and 653 and 786. The warp threads in all these specimens are particularly small, so too are the woollen threads. The quality of workmanship, together with the materials, more delicate than in the greater number of specimens, render these samples remarkable.

SQUARE PANEL, of woven tapestry, in variously coloured wools of fine thread, for a robe. Within a scarlet frame, upon which is a floral ornament, is a representation, upon a dark purple ground, of a demi-figure of Apollo with his lyre. About his head is a *nimbus.* The half of his name is indicated in Greek characters λωN, by the *nimbus.* From ancient tombs at Akhmîm (Panopolis), Upper Egypt. *Egypto-Roman.* ? 1st to 2nd cent^y A.D. 6 in. square. Bought (681 to 922, 300*l.*). 652.–1886.

See also 651 and 653 and 786.

SQUARE PANEL (fragment only), of woven tapestry, in variously coloured wools of fine thread, for a robe. Within a scarlet frame, upon which is a floral ornament, is a representation, upon a dark purple ground, of a demi-figure of (?) Orpheus, his left hand grasping his lute. From ancient tombs at Akhmîm (Panopolis), Upper Egypt. *Egypto-Roman.* ? 1st to 4th cent^y A.D. About 7 in. by 4¼ in. Bought (631 to 922, 300*l.*). 653.–1886.

See also 650 and 653 and 786.

SQUARE PANEL (fragmentary), of woven tapestry, in variously coloured wools of fine thread. The frame consists of a panelled border at top and bottom, with bud and blossom ornaments; between the ends of the borders are columns, with wreaths of leaves round them. The centre is purple, and upon it, in natural colours, is the figure of a bird (? red legged partridge), and a tree. From ancient tombs at Akhmîm (Panopolis), Upper Egypt. *Egypto-Roman.* ? 1st or 4th cent^y A.D. 8½ in. by 9 in. Bought (631 to 922, 300*l.*). 654.–1886.

The treatment of this may be compared with that in the wall paintings from Pozzuoli of about 1st century B.C. See plaster panels No. 127.–'73 to 127*l.*–'73 in the South Kensington Museum. See also textile specimens 651, 652, 653, 1886.

SQUARE PANEL, of woven tapestry, brown wool, and yellow flax, part of a linen robe. In centre a square with a circle within it, in which is a horseman. On each of the squares in outer border is fish-tailed horse and dog; above and below are fish-tailed panthers;* at each of the corners a flying woman, with scarf above her head; amongst these figures are fish. From ancient tombs at Akhmîm (Panopolis), Upper Egypt. *Egypto-Roman.* ? 1st to 5th centᵞ. About 13½ in. by 11 in. Bought (631 to 922, 300*l.*). 690.–1886.

See also Band 788.–1886, also flying figure in Band 786.–1886. The treatment of the action in the animals and horseman is particularly noticeable in this specimen. *As regard fish-tailed panthers, see scratched plaster panels from S. of Italy, B.C. 200 (?), No. 833.–'70. The women with floating scarves above their heads may be the prototypes of the ruder representations of women with scarves over their heads, such as one finds in Medallion No. 742.–1886.

SQUARE PANEL, of woven tapestry, brown wool, and yellow flax, part of a linen robe. In centre a rabbit on yellow ground; the border round it of squared vine leaves; at each corner a medallion enclosing a yellow cross on brown ground. From ancient tombs at Akhmîm (Panopolis), Upper Egypt. *? Egypto-Roman.* ? 1st to 5th centᵞ. About 5¾ in. by 5 in. Bought (631 to 922, 300*l.*). 700.–1886.

SQUARE PANEL, of woven tapestry, brown wool, and yellow flax, part of a linen robe. The frame or outer border is of a repeated wave device; within it on a yellow ground a symmetrical arrangement, consisting of large central medallion, containing (?) a panther, four lunettes, inclosing geometric ornament, placed round it at equal distances. At the four corners, between the lunettes, four smaller medallions, containing female heads. From ancient tombs at Akhmîm (Panopolis), Upper Egypt. *Egypto-Roman.* ? 1st to 5th centᵞ. About 10½ in. by 6¾ in. Bought (631 to 922, 300*l.*). 699.–1886.

SQUARE PANEL, of woven tapestry, brown wool, and yellow flax, part of a linen robe. In the centre a medallion, within a square, containing a kneeling armed figure; the ornament of the surrounding border is made up of a series of roundels with animals and human heads alternated. The edge consists of repeated trefoil motives. From ancient tombs at Akhmîm (Panopolis), Upper Egypt. ? 6th to 9th centᵞ. About 7¼ in. by 7 in. Bought (631 to 922, 300*l.*). 697.–1886.

SQUARE PANEL, of woven tapestry, brown wool, and yellow flax, part of a linen robe with rough towel facing; within a scalloped border is a band with repeated roundel and trefoil ornament, about a square containing on yellow circular ground a brown vase with vine branches from it. From ancient tombs at Akhmîm (Panopolis), Middle Egypt. ? Egypto-Roman. ? 1st to 5th centᵞ. About 7½ in. by 7 in. Bought (631 to 922, 300l.). 695.–1886.

SQUARE PANEL, of woven tapestry and needlework, dark blue wool, white and yellow flax, part of a linen robe. In centre upon yellow ground a square double-handled vase, surrounded by bands of circles and guilloche forms, worked in outline with white threads. From ancient tombs at Akhmîm (Panopolis), Upper Egypt. ? Egypto-Roman. ? 1st to 5th centᵞ. About 6 in. by 5¼ in. Bought (631 to 922, 300l.). 716.–1886

SQUARE PANEL, of woven tapestry, brown wool, and yellow flax, for a linen robe, with rough towel facing. In a central square panel is a male figure with shield and scarf or mantle; this is surrounded by a border of intertwisting vine stem, which forms large and small roundel spaces, (a large one at each corner), filled in with blossom or petalled devices. From ancient tombs at Akhmîm (Panopolis), Upper Egypt. ? Egypto-Byzantine. ? 3rd to 9th centᵞ. About 8½ in. by 7 in. Bought (631 to 922, 300l.). 691.–886.

SQUARE PANEL, of woven tapestry, brown wool, and yellow flax, for a linen robe. In centre a medallion with grotesque naked human figure, surrounded by a border of deteriorated ornament.* From ancient tombs at Akhmîm (Panopolis), Upper Egypt. ? 6th to 9th centᵞ. About 7¼ in. square. Bought (631 to 922, 300l.). 698.–1886.

* See better version in 697.–1886.

SQUARE PANEL (fragment of), of woven tapestry, red, green, yellow wools, and yellow flax. In centre was a roundel with yellow frame about it, in which was a radiating arrangement of four doubled-handled red vases, with green leaf branches between them. The square border enclosing this contained a succession of red and green vases, alternately. From ancient tombs at Akhmîm (Panopolis), Upper Egypt. Egypto-Roman. ? 1st to 6th centᵞ. About 6½ in. by 6 in. Bought (631 to 922, 300l.). 775.–1886.

SQUARE PANEL, of woven tapestry, brown and red wools, (much eaten away), and yellow flax, for a linen robe. In the centre, a square (brown), with yellow roundel, upon which, in brown, is a naked male human figure, with a buckler; between this centre square and the outer band, the ground is covered with a diaper pattern of squares and circles enclosing red crosses; the outer border of brown is spotted with small roundels of yellow. From ancient tombs at Akhmîm (Panopolis). Upper Egypt. ? 3rd to 9th centy. About 8½ in. by 7¼ in. Bought (631 to 922, 300*l.*).　　　　　　　　　　　　704.-1886.

SQUARE PANEL (part of a linen robe), of woven tapestry, brown wool, and yellow flax. The pattern (rudely drawn) of border consists of alternations of two different shaped vases; in centre are four small roundels, worked with the needle in a single yellow thread on brown. From ancient tombs at Akhmîm (Panopolis), Upper Egypt. ? 1st to 6th centy. About 6 in. by 5 in. Bought (631 to 922, 300*l.*).　　　　　　　　　　799.-1886.

SQUARE PANEL, of woven tapestry and needlework, dark blue wool, and yellow flax; part of a linen robe. In centre is an interlacing scroll pattern, outlined in yellow on dark blue, surrounded by a border of two scroll-handled amphora shaped vases, with formal leaf spray done in dark blue upon a yellow ground. From ancient tombs at Akhmîm (Panopolis), Upper Egypt. *? Egypto-Roman.* ? 1st to 6th centy. About 6 in. by 6 in. Bought (631 to 922, 300*l.*).　　　　　　　915.-1886.
See 834.-1886.

SQUARE PANEL (part of a linen robe), of woven tapestry, dark blue wool, and yellow flax. The pattern consists of vine leaf and stem ornament, worked with the needle, with yellow flax in outline, and filling a centre rounded and outer border of square. From ancient tombs at Akhmim (Panopolis), Upper Egypt. ? 3rd to 9th centy. About 9½ in. by 9 in. Bought (631 to 922, 300*l.*).　　　　　　　　　　　818.-1886.

SQUARE PANEL of woven tapestry, coloured wools, from a linen robe. On a red ground within a circular band is a male figure with nimbus (? St. Mark) with stick in right hand, and holding up (?) a green bird to a rampant lion. From ancient tombs at Akhmim (Panopolis), Upper Egypt. *? Christian Coptic.* ? 3rd to 9th centy. About 6½ in. square. Bought (631 to 922, 300*l.*). 668.-1886.

SQUARE PANEL, of woven tapestry, coloured wools, and flax, part of a linen robe. Within a dark blue frame, with outer edge scalloped, is the figure of a hare with red tongue, beneath a green leafed and red fruit branch, in the upper portion of which is a raven. From ancient tombs at Akhmîm (Panopolis), Upper Egypt. ? 1st to 6th cent?. About 6 in. square. Bought, (631 to 922, 300*l.*). 770.–1868.

SQUARE PANELS (two), of woven tapestry, coloured wools, and yellow flax, from a linen robe. Both squares are much decayed. The decoration of them consisted of a rich green central square, on which is a female figure, a *nimbus* about her head, and a fish; about this was a green border divided into odd shaped panels containing little floral sprays; the outer border was of an inter-twisting stem, forming roundels and spaces, filled in, upon a red ground, with white animals and figures (a man with bird) of different kinds, very debased in draw-ing. From ancient tombs at Akhmîm (Panopolis), Upper Egypt. ? *Christian Coptic.* ? 6th to 9th cent?. About 2 ft. 3 in. by 13 in. Bought (631 to 922, 300*l.*).
722.–1886.

SQUARE PANEL (part of a linen robe), of woven tapestry, dark blue wool, and yellow flax. The pattern, of border of square, consists of interlacing foliated stems, forming a series of roundels, in which are leaf devices. The centre of square is covered with an interlacing stem pattern, worked with the needle in single yellow thread. From ancient tombs at Akhmîm (Panopolis), Upper Egypt. ? *Egypto-Byzantine.* 6th to 9th cent?. About 10½ in. by 8¾ in. Bought (631 to 922, 300*l.*). 719.–1886.

SQUARE PANEL (part of a linen robe), of woven tapestry, brown wool, and yellow flax. The square is edged with continuous spiral ornament; the border has a pattern of rosettes in roundels, alternated with interlacements of stem (Staffordshire knot); in a roundel in centre is a dog. From ancient tombs at Akhmîm (Panopolis), Upper Egypt. ? 6th to 9th cent?. About 7 in. by 6¾ in. Bought (631 to 922, 300*l.*). 702.–1886.

SQUARE PANEL (part of a linen robe), of woven tapestry, brown wool, and yellow flax. The pattern in centre is of four octagons containing a device made up of a St.

George's and St. Andrew's crosses,* in the centre of which
is a small cross. The two borders beyond are of interlaced band ornament, worked with the needle in single
yellow threads and edged with debased trefoil ornament.
From ancient tombs at Akhmim (Panopolis), Upper
Egypt. ?3rd to 6th centy. About 9¼ in. by 8¼ in.
Bought (631 to 922, 300*l.*). 821.–1886.

* See also 633.–1886.

SQUARE PANEL, of woven tapestry, brown wool, and yellow
flax, for a linen robe. Within a square band, are four
octagonal shapes enclosing grotesque and deteriorated
renderings of men (naked) and animals, ? lions. From
ancient tombs at Akhmim (Panopolis), Upper Egypt.
?9th centy. About 11 in. by 10 in. Bought (631 to 922,
300*l.*). 701.–1886.

SQUARE PANEL, of woven tapestry and needlework, brown
wool, and yellow flax, for a linen robe. The ground in
centre is covered with parallel lines, broken at regular
intervals with small diamond ornament ; the border is of
waved stem, leaf, and berry ornament ; all outlined in
single yellow threads on brown. From ancient tombs at
Akhmim (Panopolis), Upper Egypt. ? 6th to 9th centy.
About 13¾ in. by 11 in. Bought (631 to 922, 300*l.*).
725.–1886.

SQUARE PANEL, of woven tapestry, brown wool, and yellow
flax. At four corners, within squares, floriated crosses,†
yellow on brown ; between the squares a pattern of
meshes ; in centre a diamond device pattern. From
ancient tombs at Akhmim (Panopolis), Upper Egypt.
?6th to 9th centy. About 6½ in. by 6 in. Bought (631
to 922, 300*l.*). 715.–1886.

† See similar floriated cross in No. 912.–1886. See also 717.–1886 for
similar diamond and trellis pattern.

SQUARE PANELS (two small ones, for skirt of a linen robe),
of woven tapestry, brown wool, and yellow flax. In
centre of each are yellow medallions, with brown cross,
about them are eight yellow roundels at equal distances,
each containing a deteriorated leaf device ; the edge is of
a scallop pattern. From ancient tombs at Akhmim (Panopolis), Upper Egypt. 6th to 9th centy. About 15 in.
by 5¼ in. Bought (631 to 922, 300*l.*). 694.–1886.

(*f*) MEDALLIONS or CIRCULAR PANELS (*orbiculi*) for shoulders and skirts of robes chiefly of the tunic class.

MEDALLION (for a linen robe), of woven tapestry, dark blue wool and white flax. The border, of rounded scallop shapes, surrounds the yellow ground, upon which is a representation in purple of a human figure spearing a lion. From ancient tombs at Akhmîm (Panopolis), Upper Egypt. ? 1st cent? A.D. About 7½ in. by 7 in. Bought (631 to 922, 300*l*.). 705.-1886.

This early date is suggested for this specimen on account of the subject, which seems to be a survival of the Assyrian group of Sargon and the lion, though it may be merely a typical pattern of a hunter and lion.

MEDALLION [*] (for a linen robe), of woven tapestry, coloured wools. In centre a roundel, with a human figure and bird; symmetrically arranged about it, and alternately, are women holding scarves over their heads, and (?) two columned arcades, or shrines with flower pots, beneath them. The triple border surrounding this is made up of primitive ornament, and (?) floral motives. From ancient tombs at Akhmîm (Panopolis), Upper Egypt. ? *Christian Coptic*. ? 6th to 9th cent?. About 9½ in. by 8 in. Bought (631 to 922, 300*l*.). 742.-1886.

[*] This probably belonged to the same robe from which No. 733.-1886 was taken. The figure of a man with a bird, according to Dr. Schweinfurth, probably represents St. Paul of Thebes. A square in the British Museum from Sakkarah has a naked figure with a bird, which Dr. Birch thought might be Aphrodite and her swan. In some of those circular pieces it may be noticed that the definition of the pattern is better when the shapes are worked vertically in the lay of the warp instead of across it. This is specially noticeable in No. 742, where the shrine below the centre roundel is better proportioned and more shapely than the version of it to the right and left of the medallion.

MEDALLION or CIRCULAR PANEL (for a linen robe), of woven tapestry, brown wool, and yellow flax, with waved stem and vine leaf border; centre ground covered with interlacing stem pattern, worked with the needle in single yellow threads on brown. From ancient tombs at Akhmîm (Panopolis), Upper Egypt. ? 3rd to 9th cent?. About 7½ in. Bought (631 to 922, 300*l*.). 803.-1886.

MEDALLION or CIRCULAR PANEL (much eaten away), for a linen robe, of woven tapestry, black and coloured

wools, and yellow flax. The ground of this piece is
black. In centre is a white roundel, upon which was
probably figured a kneeling human figure bearing a
vase. About the roundel were interlacing white stems
with green foliations, and within the roundels formed
by the stems, four birds, alternated with which were
four baskets of fruit. From ancient tombs at Akhmîm
(Panopolis), Upper Egypt. ? *Egypto-Roman*. ? 1st to
6th centy. About 12 in. by 10 in. Bought (631 to 922,
300l.). 824.-1886.

MEDALLION OR CIRCULAR PANEL (for a linen robe), of
woven tapestry, brown wool, and yellow flax. In centre
an interlacing stem pattern, worked with the needle in
single yellow threads on brown. From ancient tombs at
Akhmîm (Panopolis), Upper Egypt. ? 3rd to 9th centy.
About 5 in. by 4¾ in. Bought (631 to 922, 300l.).

817.-1886.

MEDALLION OR CIRCULAR PANEL (for a linen robe), of
woven tapestry, brown wool, and yellow flax. The edge
has a scallop pattern along it; inside a well marked
interlacing stem pattern, worked with the needle in
single yellow threads on brown. From ancient tombs at
Akhmîm (Panopolis), Upper Egypt. ? 3rd to 9th centy.
About 5 in. by 4¾ in. Bought (631 to 922, 300l.).

902.-1886.

MEDALLION OR CIRCULAR PANEL (for a linen robe), of
woven tapestry, brown wool, and yellow flax. The
pattern along outer border is of continuous wave device,
in yellow on brown; in centre is a diamond shape containing an eight-petalled blossom, worked with needle in
single yellow threads on brown. From ancient tombs at
Akhmîm (Panopolis), Upper Egypt. ? 3rd to 9th centy.
About 5½ in. by 5 in. Bought (631 to 922, 300l.).

903.-1886.

MEDALLION (for a linen robe), of woven tapestry, coloured
wools and yellow flax. Within a circle in centre is a
human head,* beyond are two pairs of lions with heads
turned backwards, flanking the central device; and above
and below it, on a red ground between the lions, are
? fruits on stems with leaves. From ancient tombs at
Akhmîm (Panopolis), Upper Egypt. ? *Christian Coptic*.
? 3rd to 9th centy. About 12 in. by 6¼ in. Bought (631
to 922, 300l.). 859.-1886.

* ? St. Mark.

MEDALLION* (the red ground—see 832—entirely eaten away) for a linen robe, of woven tapestry, formerly red wool and yellow flax. The pattern, wrought chiefly in yellow outline, consists of a central circular band enclosing a human head, beyond and about which is a balanced series of eight circular compartments containing animals and birds. From ancient tombs at Akhmîm (Panopolis), Upper Egypt. ? 6th to 9th centy. ? Christian Coptic. About 8¼ in. diam. Bought (631 to 922, 300l.).

830.-1886.

* This is one of a pair, of which 832 is the other.

MEDALLION † (the red ground is almost entirely eaten away) for a linen robe, of woven tapestry, of red wool and yellow flax. The pattern, wrought chiefly in yellow outline, consists of a central circular band enclosing a human head, beyond and about which is a balanced series of eight circular compartments containing animals and birds. From ancient tombs at Akhmîm (Panopolis), Upper Egypt. ? Christian Coptic. ? 6th to 9th centy. About 8 in. by 6¼ in. Bought (631 to 922, 300l.).   832.-1886.

† This is one of a pair, of which 830 is the other.

MEDALLION AND ADJOINING PORTION OF GARMENT, of woven tapestry, coloured wools. Within the circular border of floral ornament is a group‡ consisting of a man, a woman, and a child ; upon the adjoining piece are indications of a combined square and quatrefoil figure of white ground, within which are leaf and blossom devices symmetrically arranged. From ancient tombs at Akhmim (Panopolis), Upper Egypt. ? 6th to 9th centy. ? Christian Coptic. About 13½ in. by 10¼ in. Bought (631 to 922, 300l.).

743.-1886.

‡ The figures perhaps represent Joseph, Mary, and Christ, the two latter of whom have nimbi. The man has a two-pronged staff across his shoulder; to the left of it is a fleur de lys; to the left of the woman's head is the Greek letter ω; below on the right is ο.

MEDALLIONS (two, much decayed) for a linen robe, of woven tapestry, coloured wools. In centre a human head ; on ground beyond it and above and below it, two pairs of animals vis-à-vis. In the outer band are crosses set in different shaped panels. From ancient tombs at Akhmîm (Panopolis), Upper Egypt. ? Christian Coptic. ? 6th to 9th centy. About 18¼ in. by 7¾ in. Bought (631 to 922, 300l.).   671.-1886.

MEDALLION (the colour almost entirely eaten away) for a
linen robe, of woven tapestry, coloured wools and yellow
flax. The centre is filled in with balanced forms suggestive of pairs of parrots' heads, between which the
ground is sprinkled with a circle and cross device.*
From ancient tombs at Akhmîm (Panopolis), Upper
Egypt. *? Christian Coptic.* ? 3rd to 9th centy. About
9 in. by 8¼ in. Bought (631 to 922, 300*l*.). 825.–1886.

* A debased type perhaps of the *crux ansata*.

MEDALLION (in half of it the colours have been eaten away)
for a linen robe, of woven tapestry, coloured wools. The
medallion is set in a square. At the outer corners are
animals; a guilloche border encircles the central green
ground upon which are figured two grotesque horsemen
with a pair of dogs and (?) rabbits *vis-à-vis*. From
ancient tombs at Akhmîm (Panopolis), Upper Egypt.
? Christian Coptic. ? 6th to 9th centy. About 8 in. by
6¾ in. Bought (631 to 922, 300*l*.). 862.–1886.

This identical pattern appears in a silk woven specimen in the British
Museum.

MEDALLION (fragmentary) for a linen robe, of woven
tapestry, coloured wools. A human head with *nimbus*
in the centre, on red, surrounded by balanced figures of
animals and birds on green, encircled by red band and
outer yellow band with floral devices. From ancient
tombs at Akhmîm (Panopolis), Upper Egypt. *? Christian
Coptic.* ? 6th to 9th centy. About 6 in. by 5¼ in.
Bought (631 to 922, 300*l*.). 858.–1886.

MEDALLION (for a linen robe), of woven tapestry, coloured
wools, red, green, and white upon a red ground. In the
centre is a balanced arrangement of a tree with spreading
branches between pairs of lions and of birds *vis-à-vis*.†
The surrounding border is filled in with a waved stem
and scroll ornament. From ancient tombs at Akhmîm
(Panopolis), Upper Egypt. *? Christian Coptic.* ? 6th to
9th centy. About 10 in. by 8 in. Bought (631 to 922,
300*l*.). 669.–1886.

† This is a very ancient scheme of arrangement in ornament, and dates
back to Assyrian periods, 800 B.C. at least.

MEDALLION (a pair) for a linen robe, of woven tapestry
coloured wools. In the centre a duck surrounded by
balanced arrangement of ? large rosebuds and other floral

ornaments set within a leaf or bud motive border. From
ancient tombs at Akhmim (Panopolis), Upper Egypt.
? *Christian Coptic.* ? 6th to 9th cent^y. About 7 in. by
6 in. Bought (631 to 922, 300*l.*). 855, 855A.–1886.

MEDALLIONS OR CIRCULAR PANELS (a pair, much eaten
away) for a linen robe, of woven tapestry, with coloured
wools. The pattern seems to consist of a saint on horseback with a second figure near him. In one panel is a
bird. The forms are very debased. From ancient tombs
at Akhmim (Panopolis), Upper Egypt. ? *Christian Coptic.* ? 6th to 9th cent^y. About 2 ft. 2 in. by 9¾ in.
Bought (631 to 922, 300*l.*). 828.–1886.

MEDALLION OR CIRCULAR PANEL (much eaten way) from
a linen robe, of woven tapestry, with coloured wools.
The pattern appears to have consisted of a small central
roundel containing the head of a saint ?, whilst about it
symmetrically arranged were devices of flowers and fruit.
From ancient tombs at Akhmim (Panopolis), Upper
Egypt. ? *Christian Coptic.* ? 6th to 9th cent^y. About
8¼ in. by 6¾ in. Bought (631 to 922, 300*l.*).

833.–1886.

MEDALLION OR CIRCULAR PANEL (for a linen robe), of woven
tapestry, coloured wools. The pattern (in which the
forms are grotesquely debased*) consists of a central
roundel of red ground, on which is an animal. In
orderly and balanced arrangement about this roundel
and on a yellow ground are sundry devices, heads,
flowers, (?) a harpy or sphinx, animals, &c. From ancient
tombs at Akhmim (Panopolis), Upper Egypt. ? *Christian
Coptic.* ? 6th to 9th cent^y. About 6 in. Bought (631
to 922, 300*l.*). 670.–1886.

* Not unlike the grotesquely contorted details in Central American Aztec
architecture. This specimen seems to be of a period when this peculiar class
of pattern was at a debased stage, possibly therefore in the 8th or 9th
century.

MEDALLION OR CIRCULAR PANEL (much decayed), of woven
tapestry, coloured wools, and flax, with ? representations
of animals within a heart-shaped leaf border. From
ancient tombs at Akhmim (Panopolis), Upper Egypt.
? *Christian Coptic.* ? 6th to 9th cent^y. About 6¼ in. by
5¾ in. Bought (631 to 922, 300*l.*). 867.–1886.

MEDALLION (for a linen robe), of woven tapestry, chiefly
black and red wools in centre, the pattern of which consists of trellis ornament with zigzag leaf stems, in the
spaces of which are quatrefoil blossoms or crosses; the
outer border is of alternate yellow and red divisions.
From ancient tombs at Akhmîm (Panopolis), Upper
Egypt. *? Christian Coptic.* ? 6th to 9th centy. About
6¼ in. by 6 in. Bought (631 to 922, 300*l*.).   731.–1886.

See somewhat similar pattern in No. 881.–1886.

MEDALLION OR CIRCULAR PANEL (much decayed), of woven
tapestry, coloured wools, and flax, from a linen robe.
The pattern is indistinguishable. From ancient tombs at
Akhmîm (Panopolis), Upper Egypt. *? Christian Coptic.*
? 6th to 9th centy. About 9¼ in. by 9 in. Bought (631
to 922, 900*l*.).   863*a*.–1886.

MEDALLION (for a linen robe), of woven tapestry and needlework, brown wool and yellow flax. The centre is filled
with a repeated key or fret pattern, outlined in yellow
threads on brown, and surrounded by a vine leaf border.
From ancient tombs at Akhmîm (Panopolis), Upper
Egypt. *? Egypto-Roman.* ? 3rd to 9th centy. About
8¼ in. by 8 in. Bought (631 to 922, 300*l*.).   901.–1886.

MEDALLION OR CIRCULAR PANEL (for a linen robe), of woven
tapestry and needlework, brown wool and yellow flax,
with border of large and small roundel pattern; an
interlacing stem pattern covers main ground, worked
with the needle in single yellow threads on brown, in
centre of which is an eight-pointed star device, containing
a blossom form. From ancient tombs at Akhmîm (Panopolis), Upper Egypt. ? 3rd to 9th centy. About 10 in.
square. Bought (631 to 922, 300*l*.).   764.–1886.

MEDALLION (for a linen robe), of woven tapestry, brown
wool and yellow flax. On brown centre a sort of quatrefoil of interlacing scrolls outlined in needlework; the
border of yellow ground, with repeated groups of small
scroll, square and circular devices; with an outer edging
of wave pattern. From ancient tombs at Akhmîm (Panopolis), Upper Egypt. *? Egypto-Roman.* ? 3rd to 9th
centy. About 5¼ in. by 4½ in. Bought (631 to 922,
300*l*.).   693.–1886.

MEDALLION (for a linen robe), of woven tapestry and needlework, dark blue wool and white flax. A serrated edge surrounds the medallion, which, ornamented with an interlacing scroll pattern in white outline on dark blue ground, is set within a circular band of continuous spiral pattern. From ancient tombs at Akhmîm (Panopolis), Upper Egypt. ? Egypto-Roman. ? 3rd to 9th centy. About 11 in. by 6¾ in. Bought (631 to 922, 300*l*.)   692.–1886.

MEDALLION (for a linen robe), of woven tapestry and needlework, brown wool and yellow flax. The centre of medallion contains a star-shaped figure, filled in with an interlacing scroll pattern, outlined in yellow on brown ; with an outer edging of wave pattern. From ancient tombs at Akhmîm (Panopolis), Upper Egypt. ? Egypto-Roman ? 3rd to 9th centy. About 4½ in. diam. Bought (631 to 922, 300*l*.).   904.–1886.

MEDALLION (for a linen robe), of woven tapestry and needlework, brown wool and yellow flax. The centre is filled with an interlacing scroll pattern, outlined in yellow threads on brown, within a circular band of continuous spiral pattern, and an outer vine leaf border. From ancient tombs at Akhmîm (Panopolis), Upper Egypt. ? Egypto-Roman. ? 3rd to 9th centy. About 6 in. diam. Bought (631 to 922, 300*l*.).   765.–1886.

MEDALLION (possibly for a linen robe or cloth), of woven tapestry and needlework, brown wool and yellow flax. In the centre a yellow ground, upon which is a vase with vine stems in balanced arrangement about it in brown, surrounded by a guilloche border in yellow outline upon brown, and set in an outer scallop and leaf border. From ancient tombs at Akhmîm (Panopolis), Upper Egypt. ? Egypto-Roman. ? 3rd to 9th centy. About 9¾ in. by 9¼ in. Bought (631 to 922, 300*l*.).   703.–1886.

(g.) POINTED, OVAL and OTHER ORNAMENTS for robes.

POINTED OVAL ORNAMENT, of woven tapestry, in purple and red wools and yellow flax, for a linen robe. From a red, two-handled, amphora-shaped vase springs a vine,

amongst the symmetrically arranged branches of which
are a hare and a parrot; below, at the side of the vase,
is a rudely drawn (?) Bacchanal with a bunch of grapes.
From ancient tombs at Akhmîm (Panopolis),Upper Egypt.
? *Egypto-Roman.* ? 3rd to 9th centy. About 19 in. by
15 in. Bought (631 to 922, 300*l.*),   688.–1886.

The arrangement of the extremities of the branches, so that they well
distribute themselves in filling up an oval space, is noticeable.

POINTED OVAL ORNAMENT, of woven tapestry, in purple and
red wools and yellow flax, for a linen robe. From a
red two-handled amphora-shaped vase springs a vine,
amongst the symmetrically arranged branches of which
are a hare and two ducks. (The wools are almost
entirely eaten away.) From ancient tombs at Akhmîm
(Panopolis), Upper Egypt. ? *Egypto-Roman.* ? 3rd to
9th centy. About 13½ in. by 9½ in. Bought (631 to 922,
300*l.*).   689.–1886.

See also 688.–1886.

ORNAMENT (for a linen robe), of woven tapestry, black
wool, and yellow flax, consisting of a *vesica*-shape, with a
border of vine leaves; at one end a pendant stem, terminated in a small oval shape, filled in with a vine leaf
From ancient tombs at Akhmîm (Panopolis),Upper Egypt.
? 3rd to 9th centy. About 19 in. by 8 in. Bought (631
to 922, 300*l.*).   811.–1886.

OVAL ORNAMENT, of woven tapestry and needlework, dark
blue wool and white flax, for a linen robe. The ornament,
suggestive of a long-handled mirror back, is *vesica*-shaped,
with an interlacing scroll and angular pattern outlined in
single white threads on dark blue ground; at the end of
the handle is either a small vine leaf or fleur-de-lys.
From ancient tombs at Akhmîm (Panopolis), Upper
Egypt. ? 3rd to 9th centy. About 20¼ in. by 14¼ in.
Bought (631 to 922, 300*l.*).   920.–1886.

OVAL ORNAMENT, *vesica*-shape (for a linen robe), of woven
tapestry, brown wool and yellow flax, filled in with a
vine leaf, and narrow pendant band of scroll and leaf
ornament. From ancient tombs at Akhmîm (Panopolis),
Upper Egypt. ? 3rd to 9th centy. About 12 in. by 5½ in.
Bought (631 to 922, 300*l.*).   696.–1886.

OVAL ORNAMENT, of woven tapestry and needlework, brown wool, and yellow flax, part of a linen robe. The ornament is *vesica*-shaped, with an interlacing key or fret pattern outlined in yellow on a brown ground, surrounded with an edging of vine leaves. From ancient tombs at Akhmîm (Panopolis), Upper Egypt. ? 3rd to 9th centy. About 19½ in. by 9¾ in. Bought (631 to 922, 300*l*.).

812.-1886.

See also 920.-1886.

OVAL ORNAMENT, of woven tapestry and needlework, brown wool, and yellow flax, part of a linen robe. A *vesica*-shaped ornament, with stems from the pointed ends, is filled in with an interlacing key or fret pattern outlined in single yellow threads on brown, surrounded with an edging of vine leaves. From ancient tombs at Akhmîm (Panopolis), Upper Egypt. ? 3rd to 9th centy. About 2 ft. 1 in. by 11 in. Bought (631 to 922, 300*l*.).

881.-1886.

See also 812.-1886.

OVAL ORNAMENT, of woven tapestry and needlework, dark blue wool and yellow flax, for a linen robe. The ornament, suggestive of a long-handled mirror, consists of a waved stem and small leaf ornament, with a formally drawn vine leaf, fibres picked out in white threads. From ancient tombs at Akhmîm (Panopolis), Upper Egypt. ? 3rd to 9th centy. About 15½ in. by 9 in. Bought (631 to 922, 300*l*.).

657.-1886.

See also 805.-1886.

OVAL end of a band, of woven tapestry, purple wool and yellow flax, for a linen robe; a leaf fills in the oval. From ancient tombs at Akhmîm (Panopolis), Upper Egypt. ? 3rd to 9th centy. About 4½ in. by 2½ in. Bought (631 to 922, 300*l*.).

876.-1886.

OVAL ORNAMENT, of woven tapestry and needlework, brown wool and yellow flax, for a linen robe. The ornament consists of a formally drawn leaf and stem. From ancient tombs at Akhmîm (Panopolis), Upper Egypt. ? 3rd to 9th centy. About 13 in. by 5¾ in. Bought (631 to 922, 300*l*.).

805.-1886.

See also 657.-1886.

OVAL ORNAMENT, a leaf, of woven tapestry, brown wool and yellow flax, for a linen robe. Within the leaf are represented a series of ivy leaves, the two main branches of which enclose a pointed space, in the centre of which are two ducks. From ancient tombs at Akhmîm (Panopolis), Upper Egypt. ? 3rd to 9th centy. 14 in. by 10 in. Bought (631 to 922, 300*l*.). 658.–1886.

ORNAMENT (for a linen robe), of woven tapestry and needlework, brown wool and yellow flax; a waved stem with leaf at one end. From ancient tombs at Akhmîm (Panopolis), Upper Egypt. ? 3rd to 9th centy. About 8⅜ in. by 4 in. Bought (631 to 922, 300*l*.). 820.–1886.

This was part of an oval or other panel ornament for a robe.

ORNAMENT (pointed oval) for a robe, of woven tapestry, brown wool, and yellow flax. The space is divided into four compartments, in two of which are figures of a bird-headed animal and a (?) dog *vis-à-vis*. From ancient tombs at Akhmîm (Panopolis), Upper Egypt. ? 3rd to 9th centy. About 10 in. by 3 in. Bought (631 to 922, 300*l*.). 815.–1886.

OVAL ORNAMENT, leaf-shape, of woven tapestry, coloured wools, part of a linen robe. At lower portion a red flower vase, from which springs a plant in blossom, in upper branches of which is a hare flanked by cornucopia. The edge to this leaf-shaped ornament is a series of vine leaves. From ancient tombs at Akhmîm (Panopolis), Upper Egypt. ? 1st to 6th centy. About 11 in. by 7 in. Bought (631 to 922, 300*l*.). 744.–1886.

The colours in this piece are brighter than those in the majority of the specimens. They are contrasted with a black ground, and are suggestive of Roman taste.

ORNAMENT for a robe or cloth, of woven tapestry, in coloured wools, with a pointed oval disc, of concentric bands, in centre of which is a small blossom device; the disc is joined to a *tau* cross; the two emblems in conjunction being a version of the *crux ansata* or Egyptian symbol of productiveness, and typifying Isis and Osiris. From ancient tombs at Akhmîm (Panopolis), Upper Egypt. *Egyptian.* ? 1st to 6th centy. About 12¼ in. by 9¾ in. Bought (631 to 922, 300*l*.). 666.–1886.

The four armed cross and the *tau* cross are to be seen upon the robes of Byzantine priests of the 6th century. (See Ravenna Mosaics.)

U 51556. D

END of a BAND, of woven tapestry, coloured wools, and flax,
part of a linen robe. The outer border consists of a
series of differently coloured angular spaces, the central
portion of yellow ground, with different coloured discs
upon it; a dog on red ground in the oval end. From
ancient tombs at Akhmîm (Panopolis), Upper Egypt.
? *Christian Coptic.* ? 3rd to 9th centy. About 7¼ in. by
3 in. Bought (631 to 922, 300*l.*). 856.–1886.

See also the oval end of 735.–1886.

OVAL ORNAMENT, of woven tapestry, in coloured wools and
yellow flax, for a linen robe. The pattern consists of a
vase encircled by formal trefoil, branches spring from
its mouth, the neck of which is between two ducks *vis-à-
vis*. From ancient tombs at Akhmîm (Panopolis), Upper
Egypt. ? 3rd to 9th centy. About 6½ in. by 4½ in.
Bought (631 to 922, 300*l.*). 730.–1886.

OVAL ORNAMENT leaf shape, of woven tapestry, coloured
wools, part of a linen robe. In centre, on dark green
ground, a triple white blossomed (? tulip) branch,
beyond are bands of lighter green, light green, yellow
and red. From ancient tombs at Akhmîm (Panopolis),
Upper Egypt. 3rd to 9th cent. About 11 in. by 10 in.
Bought (631 to 922, 300*l.*). 774.–1886.

See also number 666.–1886.

OVAL ORNAMENT, leaf shape, of woven tapestry, coloured
wools, part of a linen robe. The outer edge of the leaf
shape consists of the repeated wave ornament in brown;
within are leaves, half of each green, the other half red.
From ancient tombs at Akhmîm (Panopolis), Upper
Egypt. ? 3rd to 9th centy. About 6½ in. by 4½ in.
Bought (631 to 922, 300*l.*). 758.–1886.

ORNAMENT or BLOSSOM, of woven tapestry, coloured wools,
part of a linen robe. The petals are red; in the centre a
yellow band, about a green ground, on which is a yellow
rosette. From ancient tombs at Akhmîm (Panopolis),
Upper Egypt. ? 3rd to 9th centy. About 3 in. diam.
Bought (631 to 922, 300*l.*). 773.–1886.

PART of an ORNAMENTAL BAND and PENDANT (for a robe),
of woven tapestry, coloured wools; an animal is
figured in the lower part on red ground. From ancient

tombs at Akhmîm (Panopolis), Upper Egypt. *? Christian Coptic.* ? 6th to 9th centy. About 10 in. by 6¾ in. Bought (631 to 922, 300*l.*). 865.–1886.

PART of an ORNAMENTAL BAND and PENDANT, for a linen robe, of woven tapestry, coloured wool; in centre of pendant a debased animal form. From ancient tombs at Akhmîm (Panopolis), Upper Egypt. *? Christian Coptic.* ? 6th to 9th centy. About 7¼ in. by 2¾ in. Bought (631 to 922, 300*l.*). 857.–1886.

ORNAMENT (for a linen robe), of woven tapestry and needlework, brown wool and yellow flax. This consists of a lozenge shape containing a roundel, with four ivy leaves pointing to centre, surrounded by sets of three vine leaves ; at opposite points of the diamond shape are narrow waved stem ornaments, terminating in an eight-pointed star. From ancient tombs at Akhmîm (Panopolis), Upper Egypt. ? 3rd to 9th centy. About 22¼ in. by 10 in. Bought (631 to 922, 300*l.*). 795.–1886.

FRAGMENT, of woven tapestry and needlework, brown wool and yellow flax, to ornament a linen robe. It consists of portion of a circular ornament with guilloche band and a waved ivy leaf stem. From ancient tombs at Akhmîm (Panopolis), Upper Egypt. ? 3rd to 6th centy. About 13 in. by 7 in. Bought (631 to 922, 300*l.*). 879.–1886.

CIRCULAR ORNAMENT (for a linen robe), with two narrow stems or bands (much eaten away), one on each side, one terminated with a leaf ; of woven tapestry, and partly worked with the needle, chiefly in brown wools and white flax. The pattern (partly eaten away) consists of a white four-leaf blossom in centre of a diamond shape, about which are small dark medallions on white ground, surrounded by a circular band with red spots, then a band of white and brown zigzag forms, beyond which the outer broad circular band with red spots on it. From ancient tombs at Akhmîm (Panopolis), Upper Egypt. ? 1st to 6th centy. About 22¼ in. by 14 in. Bought (631 to 922, 300*l.*). 757.–1886.

ORNAMENT (for a linen robe), of woven tapestry and needle-work, brown, red, and green wools and yellow flax. A square border of guilloche ornament, outlined in single yellow threads on brown, encloses four linked medal-

lions, in each of which is a coloured fruit or floral device
upon yellow ground; on two opposite sides of the square
are triangular pieces containing leaf device. From ancient
tombs at Akhmim (Panopolis), Upper Egypt. ? 3rd to
9th centy. About 12 in. by 9 in. Bought (631 to 922,
300l.). 823.-1886.

ORNAMENT (for a linen robe), of woven tapestry and needlework, brown wool, and yellow flax. A square, with
lunettes at two opposite sides, filled in with fret or key
pattern, outlined in yellow single threads on brown
ground; a twisted stem, terminated in a vine leaf, springs
from each of the lunettes. From ancient tombs at
Akhmim (Panopolis), Upper Egypt. ? 3rd to 9th centy.
About 2 ft. 2 in. by 11¾ in. Bought (631 to 922, 300l.).
801.-1886.

ORNAMENT (for a linen robe), of woven tapestry and needlework, brown wool, and yellow flax. A square, with
lunettes at two opposite sides; in centre a star device
of vine leaves, about which is a ground of interlaced
scroll pattern within a square, with panels containing
series of roundels; the lunettes are filled in with triple
grape bunch ornament, outlined in yellow single threads
on brown; one of the lunettes has a waved stem ornament terminated in a triple leaf device. From ancient
tombs at Akhmim (Panopolis), Upper Egypt. ? 3rd to
9th centy. About 22¼ in. by 10¼ in. (Bought 631 to 922
300l.). 804.-1886.

Companion piece to No. 766.

ORNAMENT (for a linen robe), of woven tapestry, brown
wool, and yellow flax. A square, with lunettes at two
opposite sides; in centre a star device of vine leaves,
about which is a ground of interlaced scroll pattern, within
a square border of panels containing series of roundels;
the lunettes are filled in with triple grape bunch ornament, outlined in yellow single threads on brown, and
one of them has a waved stem ornament terminated in a
triple leaf device. From ancient tombs at Akhmim
(Panopolis), Upper Egypt. ? 3rd to 9th centy. About
21¼ in. by 10¼ in. Bought (631 to 922, 300l.).
766.-1886.

ORNAMENT (for a linen robe), of woven tapestry and needlework, brown wool, and yellow flax. An irregular hexagon,
the centre covered with a diaper fret or key pattern, en-

closed by a square band of waved stem and ? vine leaves.
The pointed ends of the hexagon are filled in with
lunette forms, round which are vine leaves, all outlined
in single yellow threads on brown ground. From
ancient tombs at Akhmîm (Panopolis), Upper Egypt.
? 3rd to 9th centy. About 17½ in. by 14 in. Bought
(631 to 922, 300*l.*). 767.–1886.

ORNAMENT (for a linen robe), of woven tapestry and needlework, brown wool, and yellow flax. An irregular hexagonal figure with a fret pattern within a square border
of vine leaves. The triangular ends of the figure filled in
with vine leaves and terminating in a stem with small
square and vine leaf. The details picked out in yellow
thread worked with the needle on brown. From ancient
tombs at Akhmîm (Panopolis), Upper Egypt. ? 3rd to
9th centy. About 18 in. by 7 in. Bought (631 to 922,
300*l.*). 753.–1886.

ORNAMENTS (for a linen robe), of woven tapestry, brown wool,
. and yellow flax, consisting of two eight-pointed stars
with a circle between them connected by bands of scroll
foliage, similar bands beyond the star shapes ending in
vases ; the stars with geometrical designs worked with
the needle in •single yellow threads on brown, and the
circle filled in with a radiated arrangement of four
double-handled flower vases. From ancient tombs at
Akhmîm (Panopolis), Upper Egypt. ? *Egypto-Byzantine.* ? 3rd to 9th centy. About 4 ft. 7¼ in. by 11 in.
Bought (631 to 922, 300*l.*). 756.–1886.

EIGHT-POINTED STAR ORNAMENT (for a linen robe), with two
narrow leaf stems (eaten away), one on each of two
opposite points, of woven tapestry, brown wool, and
yellow flax. The circular medallion in centre, consists of
a radiating arrangement of four double-handled vases ;
beyond, in the corners of the star points, are leaf ornaments. From ancient tombs at Akhmîm (Panopolis),
Upper Egypt. ? 3rd to 9th centy. About 10 in. by 12¼ in.
Bought (631 to 922, 300*l.*). 806.–1886.

EIGHT-POINTED STAR-SHAPE ORNAMENT (for a linen robe), of
woven tapestry and needlework, brown wool, and yellow
flax. Within the star shape is a key or fret pattern,
outlined with single yellow threads on brown. From
ancient tombs at Akhmîm (Panopolis), Upper Egypt.
? 3rd to 9th centy. About 14¾ in. by 12¼ in. Bought
(631 to 922, 300*l.*). 878.–1886.

ORNAMENT (for a linen robe), of woven tapestry and needlework, brown wool, and yellow flax. An eight-pointed star.
In centre a vine leaf star device set in the midst of an
interlacing stem pattern filling a square, from the outer
sides of which, spring triple ornament of grape bunches and
vine leaf ; enclosing all this is a square band of guilloche
ornament ; the four points of the star shape contain vine
leaf devices; all outlined in single yellow thread on
brown ground. From ancient tombs at Akhmim (Panopolis), Upper Egypt. ? 3rd to 9th centy. About 23½ in.
by 14¼ in. Bought (631 to 922, 300l.).   768.–1886.

ORNAMENT (for a linen robe), of woven tapestry and needlework, purple, and yellow flax. An eight-pointed star with
foliated cross ornament in a centre square, round which
is a guilloche border outlined in single yellow threads on
purple. The other corners of the star shape have leaf
ornaments in them. From ancient tombs at Akhmim
(Panopolis), Upper Egypt. ? 3rd to 9th centy. About
11¼ in. by 10 in. Bought (631 to 922, 300l.).   752.–1886.

ORNAMENT (for a linen robe), of woven tapestry and needlework, dark blue and yellow flax. An eight-pointed star,
within which is a circular space covered with interlacing
scroll ornament, in centre of which is a star-shaped device
of vine leaves. The points of the main star shape are
filled in with triple vine leaf devices, outlined in single
yellow thread on dark blue. From ancient tombs at
Akhmim (Panopolis), Upper Egypt. ? 3rd to 9th centy.
About 12½ in. by 11 in. Bought (631 to 922, 300l.).

724.–1886.

ORNAMENT (for a linen robe), of woven tapestry and needlework, brown wool, and yellow flax. An eight-pointed
star with guilloche border worked in single yellow threads
about a yellow ground, on which is a roundel containing
a balanced arrangement of vases and formal vine leaves
or fleurs-de-lys. From one end of the star form, a waved
stem and leaf ornament terminating in a vase. From
ancient tombs at Akhmim (Panopolis), Upper Egypt.
? Egypto-Roman. ? 1st to 6th centy. About 23 in. by
12 in. Bought (631 to 922, 300l.).   755.–1886.

(h.) FRAGMENTS of bands, &c. from robes.

FRAGMENT of a linen garment with a band, of woven tapestry work, in dark blue wool. From ancient tombs at Akhmim (Panopolis), Upper Egypt. ? 1st to 6th centʸ. About 5 in. by 4 in. Bought (631 to 922, 300*l.*).
877.–1886.

FRAGMENT of rough towel material, with a four leaf device, of woven tapestry, in brown wool, and yellow flax. From ancient tombs at Akhmim (Panopolis), Upper Egypt. ? 1st to 6th centʸ. About 7¼ in. by 4 in. Bought (631 to 922, 300*l.*).
906.–1886.

FRAGMENT of rough towel material, with a portion of a square panel, of woven tapestry, dark brown wool, and yellow flax, the ground of which was worked with the needle in yellow flax, with a key or fret pattern, surrounded by a border of guilloche pattern, similarly worked. From ancient tombs at Akhmim (Panopolis), Upper Egypt. ? 1st to 6th centʸ. About 6 in. by 3¾ in. Bought (631 to 922, 300*l.*).
819.–1886.

FRAGMENT of a linen garment, with a band of quatrefoil ornament, and small pointed ornament along edge, of woven tapestry and needlework, purple wool, and yellow flax. From ancient tombs at Akhmim (Panopolis), Upper Egypt. ? 3rd to 9th centʸ. About 8½ in. by 5¼ in. Bought (631 to 922, 300*l.*).
919.–1886.

FRAGMENT of a band (for a linen robe), of woven tapestry, coloured wools. From ancient tombs at Akhmim (Panopolis), Upper Egypt. ? *Christian Coptic.* ? 6th to 9th centʸ. About 2¼ in. by 2 in. Bought (631 to 922, 300*l.*).
863*b.*–1886.

FRAGMENT of woven tapestry, coloured wools, with indications of repeating pattern. Chiefly in outline of white flax on red ground. From ancient tombs at Akhmim (Panopolis), Upper Egypt. ? *Christian Coptic.* ? 6th to 9th centʸ. About 6¼ in. by 4¼ in. Bought (631 to 922, 300*l.*).
898.–1886.

FRAGMENT of an ornamental band, of woven tapestry, worked in crimson wool and yellow flax, for a linen robe, in the centre of which are red (rudely drawn) Maltese crosses. From ancient tombs at Akhmîm (Panopolis), Upper Egypt. *? Christian Coptic.* ? 6th to 9th centy. About 5¼ in. by 3¾ in. Bought (631 to 922, 300*l.*).

883.–1886.

It has been suggested that the cross device which occurs in the outer band between the double toothed devices is the swastika or fylfot (a notable Aryan symbol) ; but this is hardly the case, as other indications of the cross device seem to show that it is merely a rude little primitive ornament and not the mystical emblem. The crosses in centre of band are similar to those used in Coptic ornaments.

FRAGMENT of a band (for linen robe), of woven tapestry, brown wool, and yellow flax. The pattern consists of a series of roundels, in which alternately are leaf devices and animals (? lion and dog). From ancient tombs at Akhmîm (Panopolis), Upper Egypt. *? Egypto-Byzantine.* ? 5th to 9th centy. About 9¼ in. by 5¼ in. Bought (631 to 922, 300*l.*). 808.–1886.

FRAGMENT of a band (for linen robe), of woven tapestry, brown wool, and yellow flax. The pattern consists of two intertwisting stems forming a series of roundels, in which, on yellow ground, are animals—dog and lion. From ancient tombs at Akhmîm (Panopolis), Upper Egypt. *? Egypto-Byzantine.* ? 5th to 9th centy. About 10 in. by 3½ in. Bought (631 to 922, 300*l.*). 893.–1886.

See also 660.

FRAGMENT of woven tapestry, red wool, and yellow flax. From ancient tombs at Akhmîm (Panopolis), Upper Egypt. *? Christian Coptic.* ? 6th to 9th centy. About 4 in. by 2¾ in. Bought (631 to 922, 300*l.*). 846.–1886.

FRAGMENT of the tapestry woven band of a linen robe, with a leaf ornament, in which is a debased rendering of a bird, in coloured wool. From ancient tombs at Akhmîm (Panopolis), Upper Egypt. ? 6th to 9th centy. About 5 in. by 4¼ in. Bought (831 to 922, 300*l.*). 891.–1886.

FRAGMENT (much decayed) of the rounded end of a band from a linen robe, of woven tapestry, in coloured wools. From ancient tombs at Akhmîm (Panopolis), Upper Egypt. *? Christian Coptic.* ? 6th to 9th centy. About 6 in. by 5½ in. Bought (831 to 922, 300*l.*). 872.–1886.

FRAGMENT (much decayed) of an ornament from a linen robe, of woven tapestry, worked in coloured wools. From ancient tombs at Akhmim (Panopolis), Upper Egypt. *? Christian Coptic.* 6th to 9th centy. About 3½ in. by 2¼ in. Bought (631 to 922, 300*l.*). 873.-1886.

FRAGMENT (torn) of decoration, for a linen robe, of woven tapestry, in variously coloured wools, with conventional floral forms and a bird (? a duck) set in half a diamond space on bright red ground. From ancient tombs at Akhmim (Panopolis), Upper Egypt. *? Christian Coptic.* ? 6th to 9th centy. About 8½ in. by 5¾ in. Bought (631 to 922, 300*l.*). 900.-1886.

(*i.*) CLOTHS or WRAPPERS.

CLOTH OR WRAPPER of linen, decorated with double bands and two star shapes at ends, of woven tapestry and needle-work, dark blue wool, and white flax. The pattern in star shape consists of a roundel, in which are well balanced vine-branches and leaf ornament; within the points of the star are formal groups of triple vine leaves; the ground, dark blue, is worked over with the needle with white lines. On each of the bands a waved stem with balanced squared vine leaves on each side of it, set between two straight lines. From ancient tombs at Akhmim (Panopolis), Upper Egypt. *? Egypto-Roman.* ? 3rd to 9th centy. L. about 7 ft. 6 in., W. about 2 ft. 7 in. Bought (631 to 922, 300*l.*). 635.-1886.

See also 724.-1886.

CLOTH, with indications of five vertical bands, of woven tapestry, coloured wools, and flax. Three of the bands were of a repeated squares* containing half diamonds with indented sides; upon them a blossom device; on the ground beyond, a red bud or leaf in centre, between two half blossoms at sides. The other two bands were of oval shapes, the bands of which are linked together in a guilloche or knot pattern; in the ovals are formal sprays of flowers; on the ground between the ovals are white leaf shapes with spotted ornament. Both sets of bands are edged with green leaf serrations. From ancient tombs at Akhmim (Panopolis), Upper Egypt. ? 9th to 11th centy. About 8 ft. 8 in. by 3 ft. Bought (631 to 922, 300*l.*). 747.-1886.

* See fragment of similar pattern on larger scale in 776.-1886.

(j.) BANDS and SQUARES for CLOTHS.

BAND (part of) for end of cloth of rough towel material, of woven tapestry, brown and coloured wools, and yellow flax. Two intertwisted stems form a series of roundels, in which were figured sprays of flowers, basket of fruit, and a fish (this latter is almost intact*). From ancient tombs at Akhmim (Panopolis), Upper Egypt. *Egypto-Roman.* ? 1st to 6th cent^y. About 14 in. by 11¼ in. Bought (631 to 922, 300*l.*).   759–1886.

* "Clement of Alexandria is the first to bear witness to the use of ΙΧΘΥΣ as a Christian symbol." (Ancient Coptic Churches. Butler, vol. ii., p. 92). There seems to be nothing, however, in the introduction of the fish in this specimen to specially connect it with early Christian symbolism. Baskets of fruit, fishes, animals, &c. are common subjects in Roman decorations.

BANDS (parts of two) for end of a linen cloth, of woven tapestry, brown wools, and yellow flax, consisting of two waved stems of foliage and berries. From ancient tombs at Akhmim (Panopolis), Upper Egypt. ? 1st to 6th cent^y. About 20¾ in. by 17½ in. Bought (631 to 922, 300*l.*).
                                                    794.–1886.

BANDS (parts of two) for end of a linen cloth, of woven tapestry, brown wools, and yellow flax. The centre part is outlined with a pattern worked with the needle in single yellow threads, and is flanked by edges of leaf device ornament. From ancient tombs at Akhmim (Panopolis), Upper Egypt. ? 1st to 6th cent^y. About 11½ in. by 9 in. Bought (631 to 922, 300*l.*).   822.–1886.

BANDS (parts of two) for end of a linen cloth, of woven tapestry, brown wool, and yellow flax. The pattern consists of repeated small roundel and diamond ornaments, worked with the needle in single yellow threads on brown. From ancient tombs at Akhmim (Panopolis), Upper Egypt. ? 1st to 6th cent^y. About 16¼ in. by 8¼ in. Bought (631 to 922, 300*l.*).   016.–1886.

BANDS (parts of two broad) for end of a linen cloth, of woven tapestry and needlework, dark brown wool and white flax. The centre of bands is plain brown, the borders on each side are of waved stem and leaf ornament. From ancient tombs at Akhmim (Panopolis), Upper Egypt. ? *Egypto-Roman.* ? 1st to 6th cent^y. About 20½ in. by 7 in. Bought (631 to 922, 300*l.*).   875.–1886.

BAND AND SQUARE, of woven tapestry, brown wool, and yellow flax, for a cloth or wrapper of rough towel material. The pattern on the band consists of linked roundels, in which are coarsely figured birds and animals and tree forms. In the centre of the square, is a radiating plant device within an octagon ; this is bordered with pattern similar to that of band. From ancient tombs at Akhmim (Panopolis), Upper Egypt. *? Egypto-Byzantine.* ? 3rd to 9th centy. About 2 ft. 6 in. by 2 ft. 2 in. Bought (631 to 922, 300*l.*). 810.–1886.

BAND AND SQUARE, of woven tapestry, brown wool, and yellow flax, for a cloth or wrapper. The pattern on the band consists of flattened roundels set between two scallop edges of leaf device'; in the roundels are animals with red tongues. The border of the square is similarly treated ; the centre has a four-circle geometric device outlined with needlework. From ancient tombs at Akhmim (Panopolis), Upper Egypt. *? Egypto-Byzantine.* ? 3rd to 9th centy. About 2 ft. 1 in. by 19½ in. Bought (631 to 922, 300*l.*). 641.–1886.

BAND AND SQUARE (part of a cloth of rough towel material), of woven tapestry, purple and coloured wools. The ornament on the band consists of an intertwisting stem, forming a series of spaces in which alternately are animals and flowers. The ornament in the square is similar in treatment ; in centre is a mounted horseman, green scarf flowing from his shoulder, with a dog running by his side ; in the small circular spaces on each side of him are lions ; in other parts of the border flower vases, hares, and flowers or baskets of fruits. From ancient tombs at Akhmim (Panopolis), Upper Egypt. *? Egypto-Roman.* ? 1st to 6th centy. About 3 ft. by 22 in. Bought (631 to 922, 300*l.*). 745.–1886.

BAND AND SQUARE PANEL (for a cloth) (?), of woven tapestry and needlework, brown wool and white flax. The pattern on square is of interlaced stem ornament, outlined with white on brown and with orange spots ; the band is of double waved stem and leaf ornament. From ancient tombs at Akhmim (Panopolis), Upper Egypt. ? 6th to 9th centy. About 2 ft. 8 in. by 2 ft. Bought (631 to 922, 300*l.*), 728.–1886.

This specimen is of coarse materials and comparatively rude workmanship.

BAND (? for a cloth), of woven tapestry, brown wool, and yellow flax, with a row of heart-shaped leaves* between stripes, on which is a guilloche pattern worked with needle in single yellow threads on brown. From ancient tombs at Akhmîm (Panopolis), Upper Egypt. ? 6th to 9th centy. About 3 ft. 2¼ in. by 3 in. Bought (631 to 922, 300*l*.). 674.–1886.

* See similar devices in 720.–1886.

BAND, end of linen cloth, of woven tapestry, brown wool, and yellow flax, with waved vine leaf and grape stem ornament. From ancient tombs at Akhmîm (Panopolis), Upper Egypt. ? 6th to 9th centy. About 22 in. by 13 in. Bought (631 to 922, 300*l*.). 844.–1886.

BAND, end of a rough towel cloth faced with flax loops, of woven tapestry, brown wool and yellow flax, with double waved vine leaf stem. From ancient tombs at Akhmim (Panopolis), Upper Egypt. ? 6th to 9th centy. About 18 in. by 8 in. Bought (631 to 922, 300*l*.). 672.–1886.

BAND, end of a rough towel cloth, of woven tapestry, brown wool, and yellow flax, with a deteriorated acanthus leaf scroll; within the scrolls are dogs, hares, ? ibex; at one end a lion; the animals have red tongues. From ancient tombs at Akhmîm (Panopolis), Upper Egypt. ? 6th to 9th centy. About 2 ft. by 19 in. Bought (631 to 922, 300*l*.). 754.–1886.

BAND (fragment), of woven tapestry, coloured wool, with a sort of chevron pattern (the sides of the chevron indented), inclosing a dark ground, upon which is a blossom device, and on the orange ground beyond, a red bud in centre. From ancient tombs at Akhmîm (Panopolis), Upper Egypt. ? 9th to 11th centy. About 8¼ in. 7¼ in. Bought (631 to 922, 300*l*.). 776.–1886.

See similar pattern on rather smaller scale in No. 747.

END of a linen cloth, with an ornament of woven tapestry done in brown wools and yellow flax, a trefoil device; a fringe at one end. From ancient tombs at Akhmim (Panopolis), Upper Egypt. ? 1st to 6th centy. About 2 ft. 3 in. by 4 in. Bought (631 to 922, 300*l*.). 880.–1886.

SQUARE PANEL (? for a cloth), of woven tapestry, purple wool, and yellow flax. The ground is covered with repeated groups of interlaced scroll ornament. The border filled with waved stem, leaf, and berry ornaments, worked with the needle in single yellow threads on brown. From ancient tombs at Akhmîm (Panopolis), Upper Egypt. ?6th to 9th cent. About 21 in. by 20 in. Bought (631 to 922, 300*l*.). 727.–1886.

This is a comparatively coarsely drawn and worked specimen.

(*k*.) CIRCULAR PANELS for Cloths, &c.

CIRCULAR PANEL (? end of a rough towel cloth), of woven tapestry and needlework, brown wool, and yellow flax. The border of the panel of double spiral devices closely arranged, and the main ground of interlacing scroll pattern outlined with single yellow threads on brown. From ancient tombs at Akhmîm (Panopolis), Upper Egypt. ?6th to 9th cent. About 19½ in. by 17½ in. Bought (631 to 922, 300*l*.). 798.–1886.

CIRCULAR PANEL (? for a cloth), of woven tapestry and needlework, brown wool, and yellow flax. The border of the panel consists of repeated five-scallop leaves; on the main ground are interlacing scrolls, forming squares, medallions, &c., outlined in single yellow threads on brown. From ancient tombs at Akhmîm (Panopolis), Upper Egypt. ?6th to 9th cent. About 12½ in. Bought (631 to 922, 300*l*.). 802.–1886.

CIRCULAR PANEL, or medallion (? for a cloth), of woven tapestry and needlework, brown wool and yellow flax. The pattern consists of a star arrangement of squares on their sides and angles, filled in with circular devices, enclosed within a border of double spiral devices closely arranged, outlined in single yellow threads on brown. From ancient tombs at Akhmîm (Panopolis), Upper Egypt. ?6th to 9th cent. About 15 in. diam. Bought (631 to 922, 300*l*.). 796.–1886.

ORNAMENT (part of) for a cloth, of woven tapestry and
needlework, in purple and red wools, and yellow flax,
with portion of the head of a female* (?) wearing a red
diadem; the left hand is holding up a cup or bowl and
an uplifted finger of right hand with ? a flower stem in
it is on the other side of the face. From ancient tombs
at Akhmîm (Panopolis), Upper Egypt. ? 1st to 6th cent.
About 15 in. by 10 in. Bought (631 to 922, 300*l.*).

714.-1886.

* The complete figure, judging from the size of the head, would have been
almost 4 feet 6 high, a sufficiently large ornament for a door curtain ; similar
perhaps in decorative intention, to such as was condemned by St. Epiphanius
when he passed through a village in Anablata in the 4th century.

(*l.*) MATS or ENDS of CLOTHS.

MAT, or end of cloth, with square of woven tapestry (much
eaten away), of coloured wools and white flax. In the
centre a square, worked in variously coloured wools, with
a human head (almost entirely eaten away) on a red
ground. The outer border consists of a series of twelve
roundels in brown, filled in alternately with formal plant
ornament and animals done in colour on white ground.
From ancient tombs at Akhmîm (Panopolis), Upper
Egypt. ? Egypto-Roman. 1st to 4th cent. About
19 in. by 16 in. Bought (631 to 922, 300*l.*).

655.-1886.

The centre is of work similar to that seen in the squares (*tabulæ*) for
robes Nos. 651 and 652. The tapestry weaving shows a treatment in
shading, and in obtaining delicate flesh tints, such as is adopted in the
great decorative tapestries of 15th century.

MAT, or end of a cloth, with square panel, of woven tapestry,
brown and coloured wools and yellow flax. The framework and scrolling stems, forming roundels and spaces
for subjects, are of brown wool on white ground; in
the centre roundel is part of a duck, of fine wools of
different colours, encircled by yellow wreath; in the
roundels at corners a dog and a kneeling figure with red
scarf; between the roundels ornamental vases. From
ancient tombs at Akhmîm (Panopolis), Upper Egypt.
? Egypto-Roman. ? 1st to 6th cent. About 13½ in. by
13 in. Bought (631 to 922, 300*l.*).   710.-1886.

The weaving in centre is of delicate texture. See also 655.-1886.

MAT, or end of a linen cloth, with square panel, of woven tapestry (much eaten away), coloured wools, and white flax, the frame work and twisting stems forming spaces for subjects of brown wool on white ground. The centre roundel contains a centaur with scarf flying back from his right shoulder; in the two lower corners are two fish-tailed animals, a horse and a panther, between which is a basket of fruit. From ancient tombs at Akhmîm (Panopolis), Upper Egypt. ? *Egypto-Roman*. ? 1st to 4th centy. About 14 in. by 10 in. Bought (631 to 922, 300*l*).   892.–1886

The scheme of the pattern and the details are apparently adopted from such as were in common use with the Romans, especially for their mosaic pavements. Drawings of such pavements discovered in Italy, the Crimea, at Halicarnassus in Asia Minor, in Switzerland, in England, are to be seen in the Wollaston Collection of coloured drawings exhibited in the South Kensington Museum.

MAT, or end of a cloth of rough towel material, with a square panel, of woven tapestry, purple wool, and yellow flax, in centre of which is a square with a naked male figure, clasping a red staff in right hand, a bunch of grapes in left, and turning towards a second figure (? a female) with scarf across her right shoulder and uplifted right hand. The outer border consists of double bands interlaced, forming a series of roundels, in which are alternately kneeling men and animals. From ancient tombs at Akhmîm (Panopolis), Upper Egypt. ? *Egypto-Roman*. ? 1st to 6th centy. About 2 ft. by 22 in. Bought (631 to 922, 300*l*).   709.–1886.

Although a date from the 3rd or 4th centuries onwards has been assigned by different learned persons, who are noted for their researches into the history of textiles and their knowledge of styles of ornament, and has been generally adopted for these Egyptian textiles, it seems right to point out that these rough towel textiles—and there are a few robes or tunics of similar material, see (No. 760.–'86)—appear to have a close resemblance to the "gausapa" or "gausapum" (see Pliny, Book VIII., chap. 73), "which was a kind of thick cloth very woolly on one side * * " it seems also to have been sometimes made of linen, but still with a " rough surface " (see p. 335, note 40, Bohn's Pliny, Vol. II., 1855). The passage in Pliny runs :—" The gausapa has been brought into use " in my father's memory, and I myself recollect the amphi malla " (probably with a shaggy nap on both sides), "and the long shaggy apron " being introduced; but at the present day the laticlave tunic is " beginning to be manufactured in imitation of the ' gausapa.' " It appears that Dr. Karabacek has also identified this woolly faced rough towel material with the Arabic " chersch," " which not only served as a " mantle in the winter, but was used in the height of summer when " steeped in fresh water to wrap round the wine amphora to cool their " contents. The principal seat of Arabic manufacture of this textile " was the Central Egyptian Province of El Fayûm."

MAT, or end of a linen cloth, with square panel, of woven tapestry (somewhat eaten away), of brown wool, and yellow flax. In centre four foliated crosses within a medallion set in a square surrounded by eight similar medallions, in which are alternately a human head and animal (? lion and hare). From ancient tombs at Akhmîm (Panopolis), Upper Egypt. ? Egypto-Byzantine. 3rd to 6th cent³. About 13 in. by 12½ in. Bought (631 to 922, 300*l.*). 807.-1886.

In this specimen a change, in style, from that in such specimens as Mat 655–892, seems to suggest itself.

MAT, or end of a linen cloth; with a square panel, of woven tapestry (somewhat eaten away), of brown wool, and yellow flax. In central medallion, set in a square, is a mounted hunter and hound. The border is of 12 linked roundels, each containing an animal, a hare, a dog, and an ibex, &c. From ancient tombs at Akhmîm (Panopolis), Upper Egypt. ? Egypto-Byzantine. ? 3rd to 6th cent³. About 18 in. square. Bought (631 to 922, 300*l.*). 751.-1886.

MAT, or end of a linen cloth, with square panel, of woven tapestry, brown and coloured wools. The framework and scrolling stems, forming spaces for subjects, are of brown wool on white ground; in centre roundel a floral ornament in coloured wools; in corners kneeling armed figures; between them baskets or pots (of fruit ?). From ancient tombs at Akhmim (Panopolis), Upper Egypt. ? Egypto-Roman. ? 1st to 6th cent³. About 15 in. by 14 in. Bought (631 to 922, 300*l.*). 711.-1886.

MAT, or end of a linen cloth, with square panel, of woven tapestry, brown and coloured wools, and white flax. The framework and scrolling stems, forming roundels and spaces for subjects, are of brown on white ground; in centre a formal floral ornament;* at corners fish-tailed animals† in spaces, between which are baskets of fruit. From ancient tombs at Akhmîm (Panopolis), Upper Egypt. ? Egypto-Roman. ? 1st to 6th cent³. About 2 ft. 1 in. by 18 in. Bought (631 to 922, 300*l.*). 842.-1886.

* See also Mat 838.-1886. † See also Mat 892.-1886.

MAT, or end of a linen cloth, with square panel, of woven tapestry, dark brown and coloured wools, and white flax.

The framework of twisted stems, forming spaces for
subjects, are of dark blue on white ground; in centre
a formal floral ornament*; at corners (?) big rose buds, in
spaces between which are baskets of fruit. From ancient
tombs at Akhmim (Panopolis), Upper Egypt. ? *Egypto-
Roman*. ? 1st to 6th centy. About 19 in. by 18 in.
Bought (631 to 922, 300*l.*). 838.–1886.

* See somewhat similar ornament in the mosiacs of S. Costanza at
Rome, A.D. 320.

MAT, or end of a cloth, with square panel, of woven tapestry,
brown and coloured wools and yellow flax. The framework and scrolling stems, forming roundels and spaces
for subjects, are of brown wool on yellow ground; in
centre roundel a formal floral ornament in coloured
wools; in roundels at corners kneeling figures, two of
whom are holding ducks, and two with uplifted hands
and (?) shields on their left arms; between these are bowls
of fruit. From ancient tombs at Akhmim (Panopolis),
Upper Egypt. ? *Egypto Roman*. ? 1st to 6th centy.
About 18 in. by 11 in. Bought (631 to 922, 300*l.*).
712.–1886.

MAT, or end of a cloth, with square panel, of woven tapestry,
brown and coloured wools and yellow flax. In centre
are four linked roundels, with figures of a long-eared dog
(? Abyssinian dog), a man holding a spear, a lion, and a
man with shield and (?) scarf, in brown on white; between
the roundels formal leaf devices in green and red wools;
the surrounding border of successive roundels (brown),
filled in with looped and square white shape, on which is
a leaf. From ancient tombs at Akhmim (Panopolis),
Upper Egypt. ? 3rd to 9th centy. About 19 in. by
15 in. Bought (631 to 922, 300*l.*). 638.–1886.

MAT, or end of a rough towel cloth, with square panel, of
woven tapestry, brown, white, and yellow wools, and
yellow flax. In the centre a roundel, enclosed by a white
spotted brown band between two yellow bands; in the
roundel a spotted animal with red tongue (? panther or
dog). The outer square border is of guilloche pattern,
worked with the needle in single white thread on brown.
From ancient tombs at Akhmim (Panopolis), Upper
Egypt. ? 1st to 6th centy. About 15 in. by 13 in.
Bought (631 to 922, 300*l.*). 639.–1886.

MAT, or end of a rough towel cloth, with square panel, of
woven tapestry, purple and coloured wools. The framework and linked medallions forming the border are done
in brown on white ground; fruit baskets, floral and
other devices in the medallions are of coloured wools.
The figures in purple represent a naked warrior, with
blue Phrygian cap and red scarf, a short sword in right
hand, with his left he holds the hair of a woman's
(? Amazon's) head; the woman is covered with small
circles (?) to represent chain armour. From ancient
tombs at Akhmîm (Panopolis), Upper Egypt. *? Egypto-
Roman.* ? 1st to 6th centy. About 2 ft. by 17 in.
Bought (631 to 922, 300*l.*). 746.-1886.

The work is comparatively coarse in texture. The attitudes of the
figures in central group are of a type similar to those of the Perseus and
Medusa in the metope of Selinus in Sicily.

MAT, or end of a rough towel cloth, with square panel, of
woven tapestry, brown and coloured wools. The frame
and intertwisting stems forming the roundels are of
purple wool on white ground, the fruit baskets and leaves
of coloured wools ; in the roundels at the four corners are
(?) a lion, ibex, hare, and dog ; that in the centre contains
a centaur with red scarf, his shield has fallen on the
ground, in his left hand he holds a disc or fruit. From
ancient tombs at Akhmîm (Panopolis), Upper Egypt.
? Egypto-Roman. ? 1st to 6th centy. About 20¼ in. by
18¼ in. Bought (631 to 922, 300*l.*). 841.-1886.

MAT, or end of a rough towel cloth, with square panel, of
woven tapestry, brown and coloured wools and yellow
flax. The frame and intertwisting stems, forming roundels at corners and in centre, are of brown wool on white
ground ; at the four corners (two eaten away) were
kneeling figures holding scarves and cornucopia ; between
them were baskets of fruit, these in coloured wools. The
figure in centre represents a man on horseback with
green scarf, beneath whom is a hare.* From ancient
tombs at Akhmîm (Panopolis), Upper Egypt. *? Egypto-
Roman.* ? 1st to 6th centy. About 2 ft. 2¼ in. by 21 in.
Bought (631 to 922, 300*l.*). 713.-1886.

* See also centre figure of 745.-1886.

MAT, or end of rough towel cloth, with square panel, of
woven tapestry, brown wool and yellow flax. In the
centre a roundel with a vase and plant, with two spread-

ing branches ; between the branches is a kneeling human figure, beneath each bough flanking the vase is a smaller kneeling figure. In the spaces beyond the circle are grotesque animal shapes, and the enclosing broad border is made up of squares variously filled in with radiating scroll devices and grotesque animals. From ancient tombs at Akhmim (Panopolis), Upper Egypt. ? 3rd to 9th centy. About 18 in. by 15 in. Bought (631 to 922, 300*l*.). 640.–1886.

The drawing of the animals is less good than usual.

END OF A CLOTH of rough towel material, with square of woven tapestry and needlework, brown wool, and yellow flax. The pattern in square consists of four medallions containing blossom devices, set in a square band of guilloche pattern, with an outer border of roundels containing red tongued hares, lions, dogs, and formal tree ornament. From ancient tombs at Akhmim (Panopolis), Upper Egypt. ? 3rd to 9th centy. ? *Egypto-Byzantine*. About 2 ft. 5 in. by 21 in. Bought (631 to 922, 300*l*.). 637.–1886.

The comparatively fine texture of the tapestry work is noticeable.

END OF A CLOTH of rough towel material, with two squares of woven tapestry and needlework, purple wool, and yellow flax. The pattern in the squares consists of (?) a bull and raven in one, and (?) a lion in the other; each set on a white ground within a medallion shape, surrounded by square border of guilloche and other pattern outlined with single yellow threads on dark blue ; fringed at bottom. From ancient tombs at Akhmim (Panopolis), Upper Egypt. ? 3rd to 9th centy. About 2 ft. 7 in. by 23 in. Bought (631 to 922, 300*l*.). 748.–1886.

MAT, or end of a rough towel cloth, with square panel, of woven tapestry, brown ground, covered with symmetrical blossoms of rude design and looped devices in coloured wools ; the central device is a square with blue medallion, on which is an indented green diamond outlined with red and white. From ancient tombs at Akhmim (Panopolis). Upper Egypt. ? 6th to 9th centy. About 19 in. by 15 in. Bought (631 to 922, 300*l*.). 643.–1886.

MAT of rough towel material, with leaves at corners, and a central device of woven tapestry, light brown and orange

68

wools. From ancient tombs at Akhmîm (Panopolis),
Upper Egypt. ?9th cent?. About 16 in. square.
Bought (631 to 922, 300*l.*).   645.-1886.

This specimen is poor in all respects ; it is possibly of comparatively
late date.

(*m.*) CLOTHS EMBROIDERED WITH LOOPED
TUFTS OF COLOURED WOOLS.

CLOTH (part of) of rough towel material, *i.e.*, faced with
looped linen tufts, and worked with the needle with
brown wool in looped tufts to show on one side only (as
in Turkey carpets), with a fragment of key pattern and
a waved line with dots. From ancient tombs at Akhmîm
(Panopolis), Upper Egypt. ?6th to 9th cent?. About
9½ in. by 9 in. Bought (631 to 922, 300*l.*).   835.-1886.

CLOTH (part of) of linen worked with the needle with
brown wool and yellow flax in looped tufts to show on
one side ; a circular ornament. From ancient tombs at
Akhmîm (Panopolis), Upper Egypt. ?6th to 9th cent?.
About 19¾ in. by 16½ in. Bought (631 to 922, 300*l.*).
                                             836.-1886.

CLOTH or part of a mat of linen worked with the needle
with dark purple, pink, and yellow wools in looped tufts
to show on one side of the material ; an octagonal ornament enclosing a star, between the points of which are
blossoms, is in the centre. The border consists of a row
of overlapping heart-shaped leaves set between two lines.
From ancient tombs at Akhmîm (Panopolis), Upper
Egypt. ?6th to 9th cent?. About 15¾ in. by 15¼ in.
Bought (631 to 922, 300*l.*).   837.-1886.

This sort of needlework produces an embroidery resembling the pile
of a modern Turkey carpet.

'CLOTH (part of) of linen worked with the needle with
brown wool and yellow flax, in looped tufts to show on
one side ; a triple band of repeated wave ornament
From ancient tombs at Akhmîm (Panopolis), Upper
Egypt. ?6th to 9th cent?. About 15 in. by 13 in.
Bought (631 to 922, 300*l.*).   843.-1886.

CLOTH (part of) of linen, with looped tufts of coloured wools (as in Turkey carpets) sewn in with a needle to show on one side only. The pattern consists of a diapering of heart*-shaped buds(?); with a band of similar devices upon a green ground. From ancient tombs at Akhmîm (Panopolis), Upper Egypt. ?6th to 9th centy. About 21 in. by 14 in. Bought (631 to 922, 300l.). 644.–1886.

* This seems to be another version of the ornament noted in 777.–1886, and in the Mosaics of the Empress Theodora at Ravenna (A.D. 547).

CLOTH (part of) of linen faced with looped tufts of flax thread, and worked with the needle with coloured wools in looped tufts (as in Turkey carpets), to show on one side only, with geometrical and blossom ornament set in an octagon in centre, and brown and yellow band at one side. From ancient tombs at Akhmîm (Panopolis), Upper Egypt. ?6th to 9th centy. About 22 in. by 22 in. Bought (631 to 922, 300l.). 642.–1886.

CLOTH (portion) of rough towel material, i.e., faced with looped flax tufts, and worked with the needle with brown wools in long looped tufts, to show on one side only; with a large hooked cross, swastika or fylfot. From ancient tombs at Akhmim (Panopolis), Upper Egypt. ?6th to 9th centy. About 6 ft. 5 in. by 2 ft. 8 in. Bought (631 to 922, 300l.). 749.–1886.

This is possibly a mantle of "Chersch" such as is mentioned in the note to Mat 709.–1886.

CLOTH (part of) of linen, faced with looped tufts, like rough towel material, and worked with the needle with brown wool and white flax in looped tufts, to show on one side only. The ornament consists of double bands of waved stem and leaf device at one end; below is a right angled form, one end of which is rounded. This is filled with a trellis pattern and below it in the centre is a circular device, in the centre of which is a four petalled cross. From ancient tombs at Akhmim (Panopolis), Middle Egypt. ?6th to 9th centy. About 4 ft. 7½ in. by 2 ft. 2 in. Bought (631 to 922, 300l.). 840.–1886.

CLOTH (part of) of linen, worked with the needle with brown wool and yellow flax in looped tufts, to show on one side only. Along one edge is a double border of waved stem and leaf ornament; towards the centre two medallions, the one filled with symmetrically arranged twisted band devices and small crosses, the other with a star figure, between the points of which scroll motives; upon four of the points are small crosses; fringed at bottom. From ancient tombs at Akhmîm (Panopolis), Middle Egypt. ? 6th to 9th centy. About 5 ft. 3 in. by 4 ft. 1 in. Bought (631 to 922, 300*l.*).   750.-1886.

(*n.*) EMBROIDERY IN RUNNING STITCHES

PORTION OF LINEN GARMENT, with three bands of diapering and square ornament, embroidered with coloured wool in a running stitch. From ancient tombs at Akhmîm (Panopolis), Upper Egypt. ? Saracenic. ? 9th centy. About 11½ in. by 7¼ in. Bought (631 to 922, 300*l.*).

909.-1886.

PORTION OF LINEN GARMENT, with diaper pattern of diamonds filled in with smaller diamonds, with coloured centres embroidered with yellow flax and coloured wools in a running stitch. From ancient tombs at Akhmîm (Panopolis), Upper Egypt. ? Saracenic. ? 9th centy. About 7¼ in. by 6 in. Bought (631 to 922, 300*l.*).

910.-1886.

PORTION OF LINEN GARMENT, with star and cross-shaped diapers in yellow flax and formal tree or fleur-de-lys ornaments, embroidered in centre of star panels with coloured red and brown wool in a running stitch. From ancient tombs at Akhmîm (Panopolis), Upper Egypt. ? Saracenic. ? 9th centy. About 10 in. by 7¼ in. Bought (631 to 922, 300*l.*).   911.-1886.

www.ingramcontent.com/pod-product-compliance
Lightning Source LLC
Chambersburg PA
CBHW031446270326
41930CB00007B/885